IMPROVISATION for
Classical, Fingerstyle and Jazz Guitar

Creative Strategies, Technique and Theory

PAUL COSTELLO

Published by Paul Costello
Publishing partner: Paragon Publishing, Rothersthorpe
First published 2012

ISBN 978-1-908341-58-7

Book design, layout and production management by Into Print
www.intoprint.net
+44 (0)1604 832149

Printed and bound in UK and USA by Lightning Source

Contents

APPENDIX

Part One: Major Scales, Tonic Chords, and Arpeggios
Part Two: Locating the Modes, Arpeggios, and Seventh Chords, contained within the five CAGED Major Scale shapes
Part Three: Adapting CAGED Shapes to create other Scales and Modes

Introduction

This book is written mainly for Classical, Fingerstyle and Jazz guitar players, who combine pick and fingers, or who just use the fingers alone. Much of the material, however, will also be of value to plectrum players. Although aimed at advanced guitarists who already have fairly well developed playing, reading and theoretical skills, players of any level will find ideas within which will enrich their playing, improvising and composing.

Although much of the material in this book is relevant to ensemble playing, I have deliberately weighted it towards the solo performer. This is because this aspect of improvisation is sorely neglected in the available instructional literature, and also because of the guitars unparallel beauty and expressive qualities as a solo instrument. I agree with Joe Pass when, to assess a students musical abilities, he would ask them to improvise a solo Blues piece or Jazz standard. This is because a player needs to have mastered all aspects of the music, rather than just the ability to improvise a single line, with rhythmic and harmonic support.

It is also worth bearing in mind that we spend most of our time as musicians practising on our own. Even if that practice is geared towards eventual ensemble work, most of our creative efforts and breakthroughs take place in the solitary confines of the practice room. For this practise to be effective, it must be rewarding and enjoyable. I can think of few things more instructional, enjoyable, rewarding or challenging as a well played solo improvisation.

In Western cultures, improvisation, up until only recently, has been widely considered relevant only to Jazz, Blues, Acoustic, and Rock musicians. However, I have been delighted to see Classical guitarists begin to take a renewed interest in this way of making music. This interest is reflected by the welcome inclusion of improvisation in some Classical Guitar exams.[1] Equally encouraging is the collaboration between musicians from radically different traditions. These developments seem to be symptomatic of a long overdue broadening of previously narrow and restrictive categories.

This book reflects a similar openness, containing varied material drawn from American and European Jazz, Free Improvisation, Classical Music, and more. My approach has been to deal with improvisation as a way of making music, rather than trying to constrict it to narrow stylistic categories.

I have chosen to notate the musical examples in both standard notation and guitar tablature. I am aware that, for many musicians who are used to reading standard notation, that including a line of tablature can be a little distracting. However, my intention is to make this material accessible to musicians from a wide range of musical backgrounds and I hope that literate players will not begrudge me trying to include their non-reading colleagues. I have also been influenced in this by some of my students who initially taught themselves to read tablature through magazine articles and material on the Internet. I was surprised to find that their reading skills were often comparable to those trained in standard notation. Although there are obviously advantages and disadvantages to both systems, and, whilst on balance I think that standard notation is preferable, I am forced to reflect on the fact that tablature was a perfectly workable system for generations of guitar and lute virtuosos.

This book is not intended to be used as a systematic course of study. Feel free to dip into, and out of, whatever engages your interest. Many of the concepts are only briefly outlined

---

1   See for example, the Trinity, Guildhall Classical Guitar Exams- *www.trinityguildhall.co.uk*

and can only be fully realised after they have been worked with for many years. Ideas that seem at first too difficult, or even irrelevant, can, when re-visited after some years, assume a new significance.

Improvisation

Improvisation enables us to create music that could not come about through composition. Furthermore, we can sometimes perform music that even the most accomplished virtuoso would find impossible to re-create.

In practice it can range from the varied way in which a good classical player interprets a written score right through to the spontaneous creation of new music during its actual performance.[2]

Many musicians choose to focus on specific areas of improvisational practice, which reflect their own tastes and cultural background. Some Jazz musicians may choose to play only Blues and standards from 'the great American song book' focusing on chord/scale relationships and song form. Church and cathedral organists improvising musical interludes during mass, utilise all of the resources of European classical music.[3] There are free improvisers who eschew all formalised references to metre harmony and melody, whilst many Indian, Arabic, African and Iranian musicians continue to create beautiful and expressive music within the framework of their own rich traditions.

Today we encounter a greater diversity and wealth of music than at any other time in human history. Contemporary improvisers are faced with the dilemma of remaining open to these influences whilst trying to forge their own musical identity.

2   See Derek Bailey- Improvisation: Its Nature and Practice In Music.
3   See Naji Hakim- The Improvisation Companion.

Finding Your Own Voice

The goal of any improvising musician is to find his or her own voice- a sort of musical individuation. I still remember turning on the radio and immediately recognising the bass player Eberhard Weber before hearing the end of just a single note. The same is true of all accomplished players.

A useful way to begin this endeavour is to make a list of the musicians who have had an impact on you throughout all of the phases of your life so far. (Ralph Towner speaks of our need to 'maintain and heighten the sense of fascination that drew you to the music initially.'[4]) You might typically start with nursery rhymes and songs you enjoyed singing at school- through all of that pop and rock music (some of which you may now prefer to forget about!)- through all of the music, you listened to because someone said that you should- up to where ever your tastes lie now.

Now you can discard anything which with the benefit of hindsight you don't like or which you identify as being derived from something much better and original. This should leave you with a rather extensive list, which you can truly call your own. If I reluctantly limit myself just to guitarists, my own list would include: George Van Eps, Andres Segovia, Jim Hall, Julian Bream, Mick Goodrick, Leo Kottke, Bill Frisell, John Williams, Egberto Gismonti, John Abercrombie and Ralph Towner.

Thinking about your own tastes and preferences in this way can tell you a great deal about yourself and the sort of musician that you are trying to become.

---

4   See Ralph Towner- Improvisation and Performance Techniques for Classical and Acoustic Guitar.

Solo and Ensemble Playing

The guitar is a wonderfully versatile instrument. We are able to adapt it to the roles of soloist or accompanist when playing with others or exploit its potential to become (as Segovia demonstrated) 'an orchestra in miniature.'

The key to being able to do this lies in our ability to adapt the same basic material to the needs of the moment.

Ex.1 is a transcription of a solo improvisation developed from a four bar section of my piece 'Graceful Dream'. It is based on the chord sequence- Emaj7#11, Eb7b13, Cm7, Cm7 and uses only these basic first position Amaj7, A7, and Am7 shapes and some surrounding scale notes, which are moved up the neck to their desired position using a first finger barre.[5]

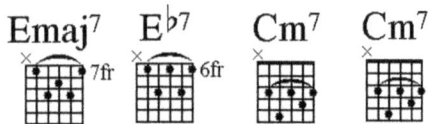

Ex.2 is the kind of part I might improvise to accompany other musicians when playing the same section of 'Graceful Dream' with an ensemble. I create the necessary textural, harmonic and rhythmic space by using my right hand to include and exclude notes drawn from the same basic 'A' type, CAGED chord shapes that are used in the first example.

Ex.3 shows the same four bars again but this time improvising the sort of single melodic line that I might choose to play when being accompanied by a pianist or another guitarist who is providing the underlying chords. Once again, I have selected notes available to me from those three basic 'A' type, CAGED chords in the 7th, 6th and 3rd positions (or from scale tones which immediately surround them).

---

5   See appendix. This way of visualising chords, arpeggios and scales across the whole guitar fingerboard by relating them to the five basic first position chord types is called the CAGED system. There are many books on the market and information on the Internet that describe this useful idea in detail. However, I would emphasise the need for us to maintain a flexible attitude and adapt these approaches to our own music and technique.

As you can see, the same basic material has been gradually thinned out in response to different musical situations. I do not wish to give the impression that we must use these different densities of texture in these specific situations- it is desirable to develop the flexibility to adapt them to all situations when the music demands it.

Chord / Scale Relationships

Ex.4 shows a common ('E' shape) two-octave B Major scale in the 6th position. The by now familiar Emaj7 chord from examples 1-3 is contained within the notes of this scale. This is a very simple and useful insight as it surrounds a recognisable chord fingering with all of the accessible notes from its corresponding key or mode. For example, we can easily identify the #11th (A#) or the 9th (F#) associated with the Lydian mode and either adjust the fingering to include these notes as chord tones or include them as part of a melodic line or intervallic idea.

Ex.5 shows the same relationship between the Eb7 chord and its corresponding (D shape) Ab Melodic Minor scale[6] (or its fifth mode- Eb Mixolydian b6). This enables us to easily include the 9th (F) or b13th (Cb) in our chord voicing, melodic line, or chosen intervals.

I apologise for the difficult key signature! You may prefer to think of this chord as a D#7b13 from the key of G# Minor (which is the relative minor of B Major- the key from which we derive the initial Emaj7#11 chord), but this still leaves us having to negotiate our way around an E# and an Fx. Take your pick! I think of this particular piece as a continually shifting sequence of modes rather than it being in a specific key. In these circumstances, I usually find myself selecting the spelling for a chord or scale, which is the easiest and quickest to think about in the heat of the moment.

Ex.6 outlines the same idea for the two Cm7 chords that are contained within a (C shape) Eb Major scale or C Aeolian mode.

---

6   I am referring here (and throughout this book- unless otherwise stated) to the so-called 'Jazz melodic minor scale', which, in contrast to the classical version of this scale, ascends and descends in the same way.

This looks quite complex on paper, but it only uses chord and scale shapes that should be familiar or at least accessible to most people after a few years practice. We guitarists have a distinct advantage when it comes to moving between different keys or modes because we can easily relocate the same familiar fingering patterns into different positions on the neck.

Ex.7 shows all of the common chords built in thirds on each degree of a C Major, C Natural Minor,[7] C Harmonic Minor and C (Jazz) Melodic Minor scale. I have listed each triad (root, third, fifth) followed by the seventh chord and finally the most commonly used upper extensions.

C Major		
Triad	Seventh	Upper Extensions.
C	C Maj7	6, 9.
Dm	Dm7	6, 9,11.
Em	Em7	b6, 11.
F	FMaj7	6,9, #11.
G	G7	9, 11,13.
Am	Am7	b6, 9,11.
Bdim	Bm7b5	b9,11.

C Natural Minor		
Triad	Seventh	Upper Extensions.
Cm	Cm7	b6, 9, 11,
Ddim	Dm7b5	b9, 11.
Eb	EbMaj7	6, 9.
Fm	F7	6, 9, 11.
Gm	Gm7	b6, 11.
Ab	AbMaj7	6, 9, #11.
Bb	Bb7	9, 11, 13.

7   The C Natural Minor scale is also known as the descending Melodic Minor, or (in a modal context) C Aeolian.

C Harmonic Minor		
Triad	Seventh	Upper Extensions.
Cm	CmMaj7	6, 9.
Ddim	Dm7b5	b9, 11.
Eb#5	EbMaj7#5	9.
Fm	Fm7	6, 9.
G	G7	b9, 11, b13.
Ab	AbMaj7	#11.
Bdim	Bdim7	b9

C Melodic Minor		
Triad	Seventh	Upper Extensions.
Cm	CmMaj7	6, 9,
Dm	Dm7	6, 11.
Eb#5	EbMaj7#5	9, #11,
F	F7	9, #11, 13.
G	G7	9, 11, b13.
Adim	Am7b5	9, 11.
Bdim	Bm7b5	b9.

Memorise these chords and arpeggios in C. Once you know them in C they are much easier to learn in all twenty-four keys, as the chord types remain the same- only the letter names change.

Chord / Scale Relationships- Limitations

Although it is of great practical value to relate chords to scales like this, I believe it is very important that we avoid the trap of applying this way of thinking in a mechanical way as a sort of solution for every occasion. A chord may contain the pitches from a particular scale or mode but be tonally related to another key entirely. Rhythmic patterns and accents can validate the sound of particular notes against a chord that in another context would sound wrong. Superimposing symmetrical patterns, the use of passing notes, suspensions, embellishment, chromaticism etc in the music of almost all great musicians clearly demonstrates the advantages of thinking of the *tonal* implications of a given note or chord. Thinking only in terms of convenient *pitch* relationships can be misleading.

People learning to play jazz for example, are often taught to use the seventh mode of the melodic minor scale as a convenient way to locate the notes found in an altered dominant chord, and the sixth mode of the melodic minor scale to locate the notes found in a min7b5 chord with an added major 9th.

A common II, V, I, chord sequence, in this case, is written as F#m9b5 to B7#5b9 resolving to the tonic E minor or major chord. Many teachers and books recommend that we play an A melodic minor over the F#m9b5 chord, followed by C melodic minor over the B 'altered dominant' before resolving to the tonic. While these scale pitches certainly fit these chords enharmonically, from a tonal point of view they are incorrect.[8]

The B dominant chord, in this case, may well contain altered notes but it still contains the perfect 5th. Even if this note (F#) is omitted from the chosen chord voicing, it is still sounding as an overtone and is implicit in our perception of the prevailing tonality. The so-called #5 is really the b13 and should be notated as such. The same is true of the other altered notes. What is commonly referred to as the b5, is for the same reason a #11. These notes along with b9 and #9 are nothing more than chromatic alterations or additions to the other seven notes of the tonic key. If we try to play these two separate scales before resolving to the tonic chord the results are invariably disjointed and dissatisfying. This is because they imply modulations that are not actually there. If we choose to use these scales because they have pitches that conveniently relate to the prevailing tonic key, it is essential to still hear the notes used in relation to that key.

All twenty-four keys have seven principal tones that have different tonal relationships to the tonic. These twenty-four keys also include the five remaining chromatic tones that also relate to the tonic, albeit in a more distant way. In tonal music, all of these twelve tones are available to us in any one key- each one having its own unique expressive quality. There is no need to make things any more complex than that. A great deal of confusion has arisen through ill informed teachers and writers trying to apply inappropriate modal ideas in a tonal context, and visa versa.

---

8   Since the development of equal temperament we habitually assume that, for example D# (the third of the B7#5b9 chord) and Eb are the same notes. This is true if we only examine the notes as measurable pitches, but if we hear these notes in their tonal context then we must distinguish between them. This fact is often more difficult for players of keyboard and fretted instruments to grasp than for singers, wind and (unfretted) string players who generally have a much more highly developed awareness of these issues.   (See for example 'How Equal Temperament Ruined Harmony' by Ross W. Duffin)

Being clear about what we mean by tonal music helps us properly understand the implications of the contemporary application of modal music and its expansion into so called atonality. The innovative re introduction of modes into European music by Debussy, Stravinsky, Bartok etc. in the late nineteenth/early twentieth century allowed a new melodic, harmonic and rhythmic freedom. Composers no longer felt restrained by the structural logic of functional harmony, leading notes, systematic modulation and so on. They could choose sounds according to their emotive impact and their colouristic qualities.[9] This expanded the way in which these modes were applied in ways that their Renaissance predecessors would hardly recognise. Juxtaposition of modal material led to a much freer use of the chromatic scale that combined with other elements, set the stage for polytonality and the serial compositions of Schoenberg and Webern.

In the USA, Miles Davies, John Coltrane and their associates also adopted modal techniques as a way of liberating themselves from the creative straight jacket that they had inherited from the previous generation of musicians. Be Bop jazz, with its overused chord patterns, melodic and rhythmic clichés and predictable eight bar sections seemed to offer them little more than the prospect of repeating the same ideas over and over again. Individual expression or development became limited to the issue of who could manage to play these clichés the fastest.

Modal improvising offered the possibility of extending and developing melodies and phrases in much more flexible ways. Pianists like Bill Evans and McCoy Tyner were able to adapt many of the harmonic ideas discovered by the European composers to improvised music. The expansion of form beyond the twelve and thirty-two-bar chorus allowed drummers like Elvin Jones and Paul Motion to greatly expand the music's rhythmic possibilities. Bass players such as Scott LaFaro, Paul Chambers and Jimmy Garrison, liberated from having to follow pre-set chord roots, were able to create much more melodic and interactive bass lines. These rapid developments in jazz seem to have had an unstoppable momentum that led to the introduction of the 'Free Jazz' of Ornette Coleman, Cecil Taylor and late Coltrane that in many ways mirrors the development of atonality in Europe a few decades earlier.

Music, like language, is in a state of continual change. The accepted conventions and values of one generation are inevitably superseded by those of the next. This is a response to the evolving circumstances to which we, as musicians, have to adapt. There are often moments during the performance of improvised music when our ear and intuition are telling us to break the rules. If we ignore these musical hunches our playing becomes rigid and repetitive, lacking all of the expressive and spontaneous qualities associated with the art of improvisation and exemplified in the music of its great exponents.

After several years of trying to ignore the advice of my teachers, I eventually made the effort to transcribe and learn sections of music performed by players who inspired me. This was a revelation. I was as surprised by their simplicity as often as by their complexity. By their audacity and courage to take risks and go for the sound they were hearing inside themselves rather than trying to regurgitate some tired old formula or bend the music to conform to some grand theoretical scheme. Once this material is familiar to both

---

9   See 'Contemporary Harmony' Romanticism through the Twelve-tone Row', by Ludmila Ulehla.

the fingers and the ears, our own musical personality will begin to gently prompt us to incorporate unexpected, surprising sounds into the music. When practicing we need to get into the habit of recognising and acting on these quiet promptings. In doing so, we discover our own voice.

Scales

When learning scales it is not enough for the improvising musician to just play them up and down at varying tempos as a classical player might do. We are after far more than just technical development here. After we are secure with the basic shape of the ascending and descending scale, we need to develop the habit of playing with it in an exploratory and creative manner. The following strategies for exploring and applying scales are written out in a deliberately simple way, in easier keys because I have found that once I have worked with simple ideas in easier keys it becomes much easier to transfer this material into more demanding keys.

I find it best to first acquaint myself with the given notes and fingerings slowly, without a set tempo. Once I feel at ease with the sound and feel of the notes, I use a metronome. At first, I choose a tempo set so slow that I do not feel in any way stressed or panicked.

I cannot stress the importance of avoiding stress and panic when practising. These emotions set up mechanical and destructive physical and mental habits which are very difficult to eliminate later on. When teaching I am prepared to spend a lot of time helping students to discover the tempo at which they can actually play a given exercise, as opposed to the tempo they imagine they can play it at. At first, I often meet with some resistance. I sometimes insist on tempos where the click on a metronome (set as slow as 40 bpm.) is equal to one semi quaver. This initial resistance usually melts away once they develop the knack of getting comfortable with the idea and then gradually increasing the tempo as their confidence builds.

Once an exercise feels easy and secure at a reasonably quick pace, I start to noodle around with it.

Ex. 8 is a simple first position C Major scale that has been moved up the neck by two frets into the second position to form a D Major scale.

Make sure you are comfortable with its basic shape then play with these notes in as many ways as possible. You might for example choose to:
a. Play them staccato or legato.
b. Play them in swing quavers.
c. In different metres- for example 6/8, 3/4 or 7/8.
d. Make up simple little tunes.
e. Outline the arpeggios of the basic 7th chords.
f. Experiment with chromatic passing notes.
g. Improvise question and answer phrases or repeatable riffs.
h. Improvise phrases on a chosen mode- Dorian, Lydian etc.
i. Experiment with extended techniques like octave harmonics, finger tapping etc.
j. Play short patterns of notes on each scale step. For example, in the key of C Major,

you might choose to start on C, jump up a third to E, and then descend stepwise back down to C, staring the same pattern on the next note, (D) and continuing up and down the scale in a similar way. You might then choose to vary this idea by ascending stepwise from C to E and then jumping back down to C, before continuing the same sequence on D and all of the other ascending and descending notes of the scale or mode. The possibilities are endless.[10]

Ex. 9 shows the same scale arranged into some melodic and harmonic intervals.

Major and minor 3rds (Melodic)

Major and minor 3rds (Harmonic)

Perfect and augmented 4ths (Melodic)

Perfect and augmented 4ths (Harmonic)

---

10   See for example Ex.48.

Major and minor 10ths (Melodic)

Major and minor 10ths (Harmonic)

Ex.10 is a transcription of an improvised idea, which is drawn from the above material. I suggest that you learn to play it as written, repeating it over and over without a break to get the feel of its cyclic nature. Once you feel comfortable you should read the following observations and then try, some improvised 'answers' yourself.

This exercise is built around the following couple of one bar motives made up of melodic and harmonic 10ths-

Each motive creates a musical 'question', which is 'answered' in the following bar. The 'question' in the first bar of Ex.10 is 'answered' with a descending scale fragment in the second bar. The 'question' in bar three is 'answered' in bar four with a two part contrapuntal idea orbiting around a perfect 4th interval. These two motives can be continually repeated, giving me the opportunity to improvise answering phrases in the spaces in between.

It is important to practise this sort of exercise in a continual loop. Over time, I have found that this hones my listening skills and concentration, and forcefully drives home the need to remain physically agile and relaxed. A metronome is a very useful tool here. Setting it at different tempos and metres can inspire totally new perspectives on the same basic material. It is also useful as a way of monitoring the accuracy of our time keeping- we are either landing on 'one'-or we are not...

When working like this I try to remain as open and flexible as I can. I may for example find myself taking a phrase that I like, and repeating it over and over. These ideas sometimes end up developing into completely new compositions, or after a short time they gradually become simpler or more complex, eventually emerging as something completely new. I may on the other hand choose to limit myself to specific notes, chords, rhythmic, harmonic or melodic patterns and try to improvise a continual stream of contrasting phrases. The possibilities are almost limitless.

Whilst it is always a welcome surprise when I discover the germ of a new composition when practising in this way my primary intention is to develop the necessary skills and tools with which I can continue to extend my abilities as an improvising musician.

I strongly recommend that you regularly record and listen to your own playing. (My BOSS Loop Station is an invaluable aid here) This isn't always a comfortable thing to do! However, we need to practice honest, balanced, self-objectivity before any real progress is possible. If you are lucky enough to find a good teacher, he or she can be of real value, helping you find a healthy balance between honest self-awareness and damaging self-criticism.

Vertical Scales

As well as visualising the notes of a key, scale or mode moving horizontally across the finger board it is also very useful to visualise them moving vertically up and down its length. This enables us to use a whole range of technical and expressive resources. Many of these (slides, harmonics, portamento, glissando, etc) are common to most string instruments, whilst others (two handed tapping, bottleneck techniques, string bends etc.) are more or less exclusive to the guitar.

When improvising, these techniques can yield melodic and harmonic possibilities that would lie undiscovered if we limited ourselves to playing across the neck in block positions. The vertical movement of the hand tends to make us phrase in a more expressive and musical way. This is an outstanding feature of Indian sitar and sarod music and is a key consideration amongst classical string players when deciding on a particular fingering for a given passage.

From a harmonic point of view, this approach helps us perceive the contrapuntal movement of different lines in a more direct way. (I will explore this idea further in the section on harmonised scales)

Ex.11 limits us to the notes found in the key of C Major. Memorise the pattern of notes on the first string. Now go back to the list of suggested approaches in Ex.8 and work with these notes in a similar way.

Continue this approach with the other five strings. Spend plenty of time on each one to fully absorb these sounds and shapes. It is important that you do this because when we move on to more demanding keys you will be able to recognise the same patterns occurring on different parts of the neck. (So, for example, the pattern of notes above the tonic C on the eighth fret of the first or sixth strings ascends by two tones followed by a semitone.)

Improvising with Motives

The simple two bar 'call and response' pattern in Ex.10 is only one of many strategies available. These are common to almost all forms of improvised music. Motivic development, transposition, ornamentation, variation, counterpoint, canon, chord progression, and so on are all of great value to us and deserve careful study and practice.

Ex.12 is an example of motivic development. It is based on the same second position D Major fingering which is outlined in ex.8

The initial motive in the first bar of this example consists of two crotchets and a minim. There is a large intervallic upward jump of a minor sixth, which then descends by a smaller downward step of a minor second-

On the first beat of the second bar, each note of this motive is reduced to one quarter of its original length. This modified motif begins on G, then makes a slightly smaller intervallic upward jump of an augmented fourth, and then descends by a major second. This approximates the original shape; making it recognisable to the listener. This strategy is called *diminution*.

The same approximate rhythmic and melodic shape is retained on the next beat, but this time this motive starts on the note A. The intervallic range is further compressed into an ascending major second followed by a descending minor second.

The last three notes of Ex.12 demonstrate the opposite strategy to diminution-*augmentation*- which as the name suggests involves the lengthening of note values and/or the expanding of the intervals that make up the original motive. Here the original two crotchets and a minim have now been doubled in length to two minims and a semibreve whilst the melodic intervals have again returned to an ascending minor sixth followed by a descending minor second this time starting on the note B. This creates a final phrase that is a perfect fourth above the original motive and is twice its length.

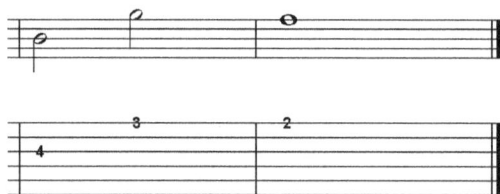

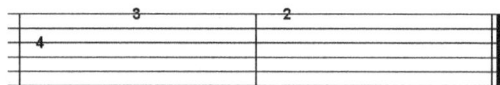

These note values and intervals don't have to be augmented or diminished in a uniform way. We are at liberty to apply this technique to all or any part of the motive as we see fit.

Ex.13 shows a motive, which has been adjusted to fit over a sequence of chords from the opening bars of the much-loved jazz standard 'Stella By Starlight'.

In this example the first and second bars contain a phrase that is made up of two one bar motives. The motive in bar one is moved down a minor third in bar three. It is then shifted up to begin on F in the sixth bar. You may have also noticed that this melodic contour follows a downward arc in contrast to the upward arc in the original motive in bar one (and bar two). Also, notice that the intervals that make up this third variation have been compressed from the initial thirds and fourths into major seconds. All three of these motivic variations are rhythmically identical.

The second of the two motives is found in bar two. Variations of this ascending two-note fragment are also used in bars four and five where it is extended on each occasion by the addition of two extra notes. The motive in bars two and five starts on the third of the prevailing chord then jumps up to its root (C# to A on the A7 chord and A to F on the F7), this is contrasted in bar five where the motif begins on the root of the F minor chord.

Doubling all of the note lengths of the motive used in bar four (and five) and reversing the initial ascending jump of its melodic contour to a descending one creates a final two bar phrase.

Once again, trying to follow the description of this example is much more difficult than its actual execution. Almost all of the notes that I used in this passage are selected from basic D shape (first bar), G shape (second, seventh and eighth bars), A shape (bar three), and E shape (bars four, five and six) CAGED chord shapes.[11]

I have chosen modal and tonal settings for examples twelve and thirteen. These same strategies are also of course an integral part of so-called atonal improvising. In fact many of the innovations of people like Ornette Coleman, John Coltrane, Cecil Taylor were in part driven by the desire to extend the parameters of motivic development. Later pioneers of European Free Jazz like Derek Bailey readily acknowledge the influence of composers such as Webern and Schoenberg for whom the motive was a key building block in their development of the twelve tone row.

---

11   See appendix 1.

Bass Lines and Cantus Firmi

A pre- composed bass line is another useful starting point on which to build improvisational ideas. This might take the form of a 'ground bass' ('basso ostinato' or 'cantus firmus'), a bass line that repeats itself continually throughout a whole piece of music, or a single melodic bass line that underpins a whole or part of a composition.

This approach was very popular amongst English musicians in the 17th centaury when the practice of improvisation was an essential part of music making.[12] It has been rediscovered in our own time by improvisers like saxophonist John Surman. (Listen for example to 'Countless Journeys' on his 1995 ECM album 'A Biography of the Rev. Absalom Dawe' or Bill Frisell's beautiful 'Throughout' on 'In Line' ECM 1982)

What most appeals to me about this strategy is its flexibility. A simple bass line can imply melodies, chords, or contrapuntal ideas that sit squarely in a tonal setting, or suggest other alternative modal or chromatic possibilities.

Working with chord structures built on top of the bass part can send the music in one direction, whilst thinking in contrapuntal terms, (whether superimposing a single melodic line or a two part intervallic idea[13]) can send it on a very different path.

This is an important principal to remember. It can help us get out of the cul-de-sacs that we trap ourselves in when we over use the same creative strategies just because they feel comfortable and familiar.

Ex.14 for example explores a section from the title track from my first CD 'Snaizeholme' ('Lydian Music' 1999) which connects a passage in Eb Minor to the home key of A Minor. Firstly, play through this bass line a couple of times.

---

12   It is worth remembering that all of the great European composers up to around the mid 19th century (including Bach, Mozart and Beethoven) regarded improvisation as an essential part of their music. With some notable exceptions (Olivier Messiaen, Marcel Dupre etc) the practice of improvisation has all but died out amongst practitioners of so-called 'serious' music by the early 20th centaury. This seems to reflect our peculiarly Western preoccupation with the written score and with academic methodology. It is interesting to speculate as to whether this has been to the detriment of this music's evolution, and its composer's capacity to communicate with its audience.

13   See Ex. 8 and 9 above.

Now familiarise yourself with this example of how I might outline the melody and combine it with the bass part and chords.

I think about these chords as being built from a series of Aeolian modes which descend chromatically from G# to E before ascending by a diminished fifth to a Bb Lydian mode / chord and then moving down a semi-tone to the tonic A minor. The melody is largely drawn from the chord tones. I have used a series of simple 'E shape' minor seventh chords using the notes available beneath my fingers to pick out combinations of chord tones and to embellish the bass. By sustaining the available barred notes and open strings as much as possible, I can create a rich, resonant, harmonic texture. I then draw out a melodic line by accenting chosen notes from within the chords and from surrounding scale notes.[14]

The melody is kept distinct from the accompanying chords and bass because I am careful to visualise three individual parts. I like to imagine my thumb as a sort of 'poor man's double bass' and the chords played on the middle strings as 'piano chords'. The melody is made up of a short motive that moves and develops with the changing harmony.[15] I am trying to maintain a conversation between the three parts.

Try using the same sequence of chords to improvise alternative solo guitar versions of the same idea. Use the same E and A shape CAGED chords to begin with, staying fairly close

14   See Ex.1-7
15   See Ex. 11 and 12

to the version given in Ex.14. Make just small variations to the original.[16]

Once you get used to this, start using alternative CAGED[17] voicings of the same chords. These alternative chord voicings, on different parts of the neck allow you to reconfigure the bass part in different octaves. They give variety to the sound of the chord's inner voices, and, most importantly, enable you to reconstruct the melody by placing different chord tones on the top two or three strings.

Ex.14.1 shows this same chord sequence using an E shape G#m9, a D shape Gm7, a C shape Fm9 (this one is a little difficult to see at first), an A shape Fm7, a G shape Emb6 (again, difficult to categorise- try outlining the arpeggio starting with the fourth finger on the E on the sixth string, twelfth fret and it should be more clear) and a D shape Bbmaj7.

Notice how the highest notes of each chord suggest an alternative melodic contour. Notice also, how in the first five bars, the bass line descends, whilst the melodic notes on the top of these chords ascend. This illustrates the idea of contrary motion, which will be explored later in Ex.16.

I have also added occasional extensions to these basic chords (9ths and a b6) to introduce more harmonic colour and to extend my melodic choices.

Ex.15 uses the same bass line and modal sequence as Ex.14, but rather than thinking in terms of chords I am utilising intervals drawn from each successive mode to create a contrapuntal texture.[18]

---

16   Pianist Keith Jarrett recalls his own earliest improvisation as consisting of nothing more than the addition of a single note to the end of a piece by Bach.

17   See appendix 1.

18   See Ex.9 and 10

This is not the strict 'species counterpoint' Outlined by Joseph Fux in his famous 1775 treatise 'Gradus ad Parnassum'- and still taught to students of composition today. It would be impractical for us to try to apply these rigorous rules when improvising.[19] Instead we need to prepare ourselves for the moment by becoming thoroughly familiar with the shapes and sounds of all of the intervals and scales in all twenty-four keys, so that we can utilise them in a spontaneous and intuitive way.

It is also important to get used to using a variety of different directions in the lines that you improvise.

Ex.16 outlines the four basic types of contrapuntal movement.

1. Parallel motion: when all of the voices move in the same direction, keeping the same distance apart.

2. Similar motion: when the voices move in the same direction but the intervals between them differ.

---

19   For a thorough exploration of this useful, complex and engrossing subject I strongly recommend Dusan Bogdanovic's excellent 'Counterpoint For Guitar'.

3. Contrary motion: when the voices move in opposite directions.

4. Oblique motion: when one of the voices stays in the same place whilst the other voice or voices move towards or away from it.

For the sake of clarity I have chosen to use only two voices moving in semibreves in the first position. Clearly it is possible, with practise, to use three or more voices combined with any combination of note values over the whole fingerboard, however it is all to easy when attempting to work with these complex ideas to get very quickly out of our depth. The trick is to start out simply and graduate to more complex ideas only as our brains become able to process the information without us getting flustered and disorientated.

An essential element in this process is space. Just as in a good conversation, each participant needs the space in which to express themselves, so each of these musical voices must leave space for the others. As the melody is usually the most important element in the music, I tend to focus on this first, allowing the other voices to find their own spaces as the melody unfolds. However, generalisations are dangerous and if we overuse any one strategy or use it in a mechanical way, the music dies. Bass lines can evolve a melodic momentum of their own and become the focus of attention. Shifting harmonies and arpeggio patterns can become so compelling during the course of an improvisation that they in turn demand all of our attention at the expense of all else. Good improvisers are able to remain alert to the possibilities of each passing moment, and have learnt to remain flexible enough to respond to these possibilities as they occur.

I also think it is important to stress, in this context, the need to play within our own limitations when improvising. Trying to use techniques and ideas that have yet to become assimilated as a fluent part of our own musical vocabulary can only inhibit the flow of ideas. Some of the greatest improvising musicians have had only relatively modest technical resources. What makes them great is that they are able to use these limited means to make music that is coherent and meaningful. This is contrasted by musicians, of sometimes mind-boggling technical ability, who manage to produce only incoherent, insincere and trivial music.

Ex.17 shows two examples of Cantus Firmi. I have shown each one as both a lower and an upper voice.

The first examples are in C Major:

Lower voice.

Upper voice.

The second are in the E Phrygian mode:

Lower voice.

Upper voice.

Although it is tempting and useful to harmonise these lines with our familiar root position and inverted chords, (see 'Harmonised Scales' below) we lose nothing, and gain a great deal through learning to compose and improvise in a contrapuntal way. When I am performing solo, counterpoint greatly enriches the musical resources that I can call upon- enabling me to introduce a much more varied and interesting texture than I could achieve by relying only on chords, arpeggios and scales.

When playing in a group I find that counterpoint is a refreshing alternative to the usual chordal approach adopted by most players. I have also noticed that many transcriptions of music by contemporary jazz guitarists like John Abercrombie, Jim Hall or Bill Frisell often interpret their harmonies as very complex chords. Closer inspection reveals that the musician in question is sometimes thinking less in terms of chords, and more in terms of counterpoint.

With only six strings at our disposal, we can't hope to emulate the harmonic complexity that is so readily available to pianists and harpists. However, the guitars, varied timbre and its unparalleled expressive resources means that even simple intervals, which sound unremarkable on these instruments can sound rich and complete in themselves when played on the guitar. With a little knowledge and care, we can give the impression of much more with much less.

Ex.18 is an example of how I might use this approach to accompany the first eight bars from the beautiful Bill Evans ballad 'Turn Out The Stars'. You can find the melody in many of the available fake books. Bill recorded the piece a few times. My own favourite version is the one he recorded as a duet with Jim Hall on the album 'Intermodulation'.

Because the part consists of only two voices, it maintains much more clarity and rhythmic flexibility than a part consisting of those more familiar, larger chord shapes. It is also less likely to clutter the overall sound or clash with the melodic or bass parts.

Understandably, improvising like this appears at first to be a rather daunting task. However, it is important to bear in mind that I am only re-assembling already familiar patterns and shapes. For example, I borrowed convenient intervals from some of the basic chord voicings that George Van Eps memorably used to call 'old friends'. I then connected these together using mostly sixths and thirds[20] taken from the prevailing keys,[21]adding chromatic passing notes to smooth out the lines and add variety. (See for example the C# in bar two, the Ab in bar three and the Db in bar five.) For extra bite, I played occasional tri-tones in cadential areas. For the same reason I used an augmented second in bar three and an unusual diminished octave in bar one.

Get used to using as wide a variety of intervals as possible. They are all useful. Seconds, sevenths and ninths and tri-tones all have a dissonant 'outside' quality. Fourths and fifths have a consonant, hollow quality that enables them to easily drift in between keys. Close intervals that sound dissonant sound more consonant when separated by an octave. Major and minor thirds, and sixths are inversions of each other. I use these as basic building blocks. It is possible to play them in long unbroken lines, achieving variety by alternating between them. Separated by an octave they become rich and sonorous tenths and thirteenths. These intervals have so much 'weight' that they could almost be taken as chords in their own right and I often find myself using them in this way.

Try alternating different intervals to create more interesting movement between separate lines. I find it useful to practise embellishing either the upper or lower voice of the interval with neighbouring diatonic or chromatic scale tones.

I suggest that you start working on the following assignments. Take your time with each one, and try to resist the temptation to move on to another before properly mastering it.

- a. Compose and memorise a cantus firmus as both an upper and lower voice in common time, using ex 16 as a model. Use only semibreves and keep it in a guitar friendly key like C or G major, or A and E minor (or one of the associated modes).
- b. Setting your metronome at a very slow tempo and playing only notes from the chosen key, practise improvising different versions of the four types of contrapuntal motion outlined in example fifteen. When you find one you like write it down.
- c. Using these written parts try embellishing either the upper or lower line by dividing each semibreve into two minims, then four crotchets, then eight quavers, then sixteen semiquavers. Be sure to keep in time with the metronome and make the first interval you play in each bar the same as in the original written part; improvising a line that leads nicely into the first two notes of the next bar.
- d. Get used to cycling these sequences around and around, aiming for a smooth, relaxed continuity in your improvised line and a nice solid consistent second part.
- e. Now try mixing together different note values. (Quavers with minims, crotchets with semiquavers etc)
- f. Once you feel comfortable with all of these exercises I suggest that you experiment by starting one or both lines on different beats of the bar. Try superimposing melodic and harmonic intervals rather than just single lines and gradually introduce new time signatures, tied notes and rests to provide rhythmic variety.
- g. Play through Renaissance and Baroque lute and vihuela transcriptions. When you are familiar with the melody, harmony and form of a piece try improvising new

---

20   See Ex.9
21   Two bars of A minor followed by two bars each of C, Eb and G major.

versions. You don't need to make radical changes at first. Even small alterations and embellishments are very satisfying to play and can yield valuable insights. It is also worth remembering that the musicians who originally created and performed this music would have used a similar approach.

Improvisation and Composition

I have found the classical guitar repertoire to be an invaluable source of ideas, information and inspiration throughout my musical life, and yet the practice of improvisation amongst classical musicians has been sadly neglected. The reasons for this are difficult to understand, bearing in mind its central role in European music right up to the Romantic period.[22]

Music, along with the arts in general, is a product of its time and culture. Modernism and the late romantic periods are distinguished by a preoccupation with the ideal of the artist as a unique heroic, creative genius. This figure was inevitably a white male who asserted absolute control over the performance of his work through the printed score. Throughout the late nineteenth and into the twentieth century an increasingly rigid and dogmatic academic outlook dominated 'serious' music. These attitudes combined with political and cultural prejudices that were dismissive of music and musicians who did not conform to its own ideals. Improvisation was often denigrated by musicians who because of their background and training were unable to improvise themselves and had no idea of its possibilities. The most obvious and well-documented example of this is in the reactions of critics and the musical establishment as a whole towards jazz. These attitudes still unfortunately exist today. I was recently told of a conversation with a classical violinist who, when the subject of improvisation came up pronounced in a dismissive tone, 'Oh, you mean busking!'

Fortunately, improvisation is once again becoming more accepted amongst classical guitarists[23] and in the classical music world as a whole. (It has, for example, recently been introduced as an optional part of the Trinity College of Music exams and in some of the more forward thinking college and university courses) Guitarists from a jazz background like George Van Eps, Charlie Byrd, Lenny Breau and Earl Klugh have been greatly influenced by classical guitar, and their music, books, interviews etc. have a great deal to offer classical musicians who wish to learn how to improvise. The Brazilian composer/pianist/guitarist, Egberto Gismonti and American composer/guitarist/pianist Ralph Towner are both accomplished classical musicians who have managed to re-unite these different approaches in their own unique ways.

In music simple ideas, when you start to combine them, tend to become very complex very quickly. The advantage of composing over improvising is that we can spend as much time as we want in considering and reconsidering this multitude of options before we have to decide on the final shape of the finished score. As improvisers we simply don't have the time to do this. Decisions, which will go on to determine the success or failure of the piece, have to be made in an instant.

It would be easy to conclude from this that a purely compositional approach to creating music will automatically yield the best results. This argument is difficult to sustain however, when we take into account improvisations continuous use in all cultures throughout history. Even if we narrow our focus to purely European culture in the last few centuries, we can find ample evidence to support its teaching and practice. It is a matter of historical record, for example, that Frederic Chopin's piano improvisations were held in higher esteem (by those

---

22   J S Bach, Handel, Mozart, Beethoven, Corelli, Hummel, Liszt, Frank, Bruckner, and Chopin for example all regarded improvisation as an integral element in their music.

23   See 'Ex Ovo- A guide for perplexed composers and improvisers' by Dusan Bogdanovic.

lucky enough to have heard them) than his written compositions[24], and we may wonder as to what advantages Mozart, Beethoven and their contemporaries saw in improvising a cadenza rather than relying on a written part.

I think that this question can be answered by taking into account some intriguing insights that contemporary science is beginning to give us into the nature of our own minds. The American writer and thinker Malcolm Gladwell in his book 'Blink' has provided us with several compelling examples of people who in the course of their professional lives rely on the ability to make very complex decisions in an instant. Furthermore he points out that certain tasks that demand a fluid, intuitive, non-verbal approach are inhibited if we try to become reflective or think in an analytical or systematic way. It seems that trying to impose preconceptions and pre- learnt models of behaviour and thinking short circuit the very flexibility and spontaneity that is essential for success in these sorts of activities. This can be seen in all sorts of areas of life. A professional footballer, for example, does not start trying to make involved calculations about velocity, wind speed and the weight of the ball before taking a crucial free kick. A pilot landing an airliner in a storm would crash it if he suddenly decided to start systematically processing all of the information from his instrument panel, rather than relying on his experience and intuitive skill to co-ordinate the multiplicity of relevant factors at the right moment.

Recent research in cognitive science suggests that we have extensive mental capacities that lie beneath the surface of our conscious intellect. These more subtle layers of mind are, in certain ways, more capable of navigating the intricacies of creating music, diagnosing illness, or solving complex scientific questions than our more familiar thought processes. This form of intelligence does not involve the deliberate application of logic and sequential thought that is so highly valued in our own present culture. It is more akin to the contemplative non-verbal, intuitive modes of thought commonly associated with eastern cultures. Professor Guy Claxton in his book 'Hare Brain Tortoise Mind- Why Intelligence Increases When You Think Less', details the growing body of empirical evidence that points the way to a (for us) totally new way of understanding our own thought processes.

I suspect that poets, scientists, craftsmen, mathematicians, musicians and the like have always sensed this. The great guitar maker Antonio De Torres, when pressed to reveal the secret of his wonderful instruments insisted that it would accompany him to his grave-not because he refused to discuss the processes of guitar making with interested enquirers, but because it lay in the 'feel' of the wood between his thumb and index finger. The arts and sciences (and many other areas of life) are full of comparable accounts of this type of intuitively lead thought and action. Putting to one side for a moment the far reaching implications of these ideas for our culture as a whole, I believe that this line of enquiry can yield important clues as to the nature and role of improvisation in music making as well as the way in which it can be taught and practiced.

Group interaction is another important feature in the creation of improvised music that has no bearing on the work of the solitary composer. Anybody watching an improvised

---

24   'and the few lucky ones who have heard him improvising...- those people will agree with us in saying that Chopin's most beautiful finished compositions are merely reflections and echoes of his improvisations.' (Jules Fontana [preface to] 'Oeuvres posthumes pour piano de Fred. Chopin'. Paris, Meissonnier [1855], 8 vols.) Quoted in 'Chopin, Pianist and Teacher', by Jean-Jacques Eigeldinger.

performance by a jazz quartet or an Indian classical music ensemble cannot help but notice the way in which the interaction between the individual participants actually shapes the music as it is being created. Less often commented upon is the influence of the audience on the performers and their creative choices.[25]

Once again, contemporary science yields valuable insights into this unique element in improvised music. We are now becoming aware of the surprising fact that the vast bulk of interaction and communication between people is non-verbal and registered at an unconscious rather than conscious level. This includes the previously unsuspected synchronisation of tiny unconscious rhythmic gestures and eye movements and even patterns of co-ordinated brain activity. Clearly, these findings have far reaching implications for musicians and audiences, and for society as a whole. It is beyond the scope of this book to explore these findings in the detail they deserve. I thoroughly recommend the books of the eminent American anthropologist Edward T Hall in which he outlines the fruits of a lifetime's work in this area.[26]

All of the factors noted above constitute compelling reasons for us to value the important and unique role of improvisation in our musical culture.

The language we use when discussing these ideas tends to leave the impression that these two ways of creating music represent opposite, irreconcilable poles. This is clearly not the case. The classical performer must interpret, in a uniquely personal way, even the most detailed score, which includes precise directions as to every nuance of articulation and dynamics. The same piece of music sounds different every time it is performed- even when played by the same musician.

It is also debatable whether there can be such a thing as pure improvisation. All improvising players find themselves using pre-learnt strategies and patterns that they adapt to the needs of the moment. Much music that is categorised as improvised contains, to varying degrees, significant sections that are pre-composed. The music of Duke Ellington is a good example of large scale, complex compositions that, at key points exploit the energy and spontaneity of his musicians improvising skills. John Coltrane's 'A Love Supreme' is often regarded as a model of 'free' jazz playing and yet it contains significant pre-determined elements that underpin all four sections of the piece.[27] The music of Ornette Coleman, Cecil Taylor and later generations of players who have dedicated themselves to the idea of free improvisation still frame their music in an admittedly personalised 'language'- but a language none the less- With all of the implicit musical vocabulary, repeated structures and 'signature phrases'.

It seems most helpful to think of any piece of music as occupying some point on a spectrum between 'pure' composition and 'pure' improvisation.

25   See for example 'Thinking in Jazz' by Paul F Berliner- essential reading for anyone interested in jazz and improvised music.

26   See for example 'The Dance of Life', 'The Silent Language' or 'The Hidden Dimension'.

27   See 'John Coltrane- His Life and Music' by Lewis Porter.

Chord Scales

Chord scales are of great value to all guitarists, and especially to those who take up the formidable challenges of solo performance. They offer distinct advantages when playing purely melodic and harmonic ideas and, crucially for those of us utilising classical and fingerstyle technique, enable us to combine both melody and harmony. If this material is new to you, it will take some time and effort to assimilate it to the point when it can be applied in a fluent and confident way- but I would really encourage you to persevere. The rewards of all of this effort are well worth it.

Chord scales are the missing link between chords, arpeggios and scales. Virtually all of the available instructional literature on guitar improvisation is either aimed at, or derived from, plectrum style jazz Guitar.[28] As a consequence, these books tend to separate scale derived melodic playing and block chord type 'comping'. This is understandable as these strategies exploit the strengths of this style and avoid its inherent weaknesses, however I think that this situation has tended to condition and limit the imagination of everyone else, brainwashing us into a creative straight jacket. Perhaps the best example of this is Joe Pass, (whose music I like and admire) and the many players who have since adopted his approach.

It is interesting to note the amount of great players who started with a plectrum and gradually evolved towards using their fingers. Joe Pass gradually dispensed with the plectrum, abandoning it almost completely in the last few years of his life. George Van Eps made a similar decision, but much earlier in his career. I notice that John Abercrombie seems to be moving in a similar direction. More surprising are rock players, like Jeff Beck, Pete Townsend and Mark Knopfler.

Playing with the fingers facilitates much more harmonic and contrapuntal variety and sophistication. Melodically it enables us to exploit wider intervals more easily. We can utilise the most complex and intriguing polyrhythms, as exemplified by guitarists like Ali Farka Toure, and incorporate all of the virtuosity of classical and flamenco technique. The combination of nail and flesh and the contrast between thumb and different fingers gives us an extended palette of tone colours to choose from.

The following exercises are intended to outline only some of the myriad of possibilities of this line of thought, and to stimulate your own curiosity and research. It is not my intention to detail all of the possibilities in every key, but to give you starting points which you can familiarise yourself with and learn to apply. I have found that once I can use a particular idea in one key, it is then a much simpler matter to start applying it to different keys. Patterns and shapes relate to each other in symmetrical ways that are relatively easy to visualise and to transfer to different positions on the neck.

---

28   Notable exceptions include books by George Van Eps, Ted Green, Ralph Towner, Mick Goodrick and Alan De Mause.

Ex.19 shows first and second inversion triads in the key of C Major.
First inversion.

Second inversion.

Memorise these shapes and play them in ascending and descending patterns. Start with simple stepwise movements, and then try moving up and down in thirds, graduating to larger intervallic leaps and more complex combinations as you become more confident with the material. When you can do this fluently, try working with the following suggestions:

a. Improvise simple melodic phrases, still in block chords.
b. Vary your right hand fingering and try to get used to moving smoothly from any one chord to any other.
c. Orbit your improvisations around different chords to suggest any one of the seven different modes available.[29]
d. Break up the block chords into arpeggios to introduce more rhythmic and melodic variety.
e. Experiment with right hand position, and the angle of attack of the fingernails to introduce more tone colours.
f. Practise the triads using natural and artificial harmonics.

Ex.19.1 is a transcription of an improvised phrase using some of the first inversion triads from Ex.19. It is based on C, F and G triads that orbit around a D minor triad- suggesting the Dorian mode.

---

29   Ionian (major scale), Dorian, Phrygian, Lydian, Mixolydian, Aeolian (natural minor), Locrian.

Ex19.2 takes the same triads and develops them into a melodic line. You will notice when playing this example, that an impression of the original chords is retained. This is a consequence of the guitars natural resonance and unique fingering possibilities. Individual notes can be allowed ring over, implying a rich harmonic texture with only a limited amount of notes. This impression of suggesting 'more with less' is further developed through the use of vibrato, slides, portamento and so on. As with the previous example, use *p* on the lower note of each triad, and *i* and *m* for the middle and upper notes.

Ex.20 shows the same first and second inversion triads ascending vertically on each separate group of three strings. These should be practiced in the same way as in the previous exercise.

First inversion- strings four, five and six.

Second inversion- strings four, five and six.

First inversion- strings three, four and five.

Second inversion- strings three, four and five.

First inversion- strings two, three and four.

Second inversion- strings two, three and four.

First inversion- strings one, two and three.

Second inversion- strings one, two and three.

Although root position triads are obviously important, I have focused on first and second inversion triads in these exercises because I find them more flexible and useful for melodic playing, and for adding extensions to basic chords. I am also assuming that, as a more advanced player, you already know them.

Ex.21 shows first and second inversion triads from a C (jazz) Melodic Minor scale and a C Harmonic Minor scale.

First inversion- C Melodic Minor.

Second inversion- C Melodic Minor.

First inversion- C Harmonic Minor.

Second inversion- C Harmonic Minor.

Although the key signature and accidentals are essential when thinking in terms of a key, they are not essential when applying the scale in a modal or chromatic way. What does matter to the improvising player is how quickly he or she can apply these strategies in a practical way during the actual performance of the music. I think you will agree that it is easier to think of C Melodic Minor as a C Major scale with a b3rd, rather than try to work out the relative minor of Eb Major and the raise the 6th and 7th degrees by a semitone. In a similar way we can think of D Melodic Minor, and its other six modes, as a C Major scale with the C raised to C#. (Think- D Dorian mode- the second mode of C Major- with a #7th)

It is useful to be able to think quickly about modes and scales from different perspectives. For example the F Lydian mode could be thought of as the fourth mode of C Major, or as an F Major scale with its 4th degree (Bb) raised by a semitone to B. An F Mixolydian mode can be thought of as an F Major scale with a b7th degree (E-Eb), or as an F Dorian mode with a raised 3rd. (Ab- A). A Harmonic Minor scale is an Aeolian mode (or Natural Minor scale) with a raised 7th, and so on.

Once you have become thoroughly familiar with these triad shapes in the keys of C Major and Minor, you should then practise them all one fret higher in the keys of Db major and minor.

In a similar way, you should gradually acquaint yourself with these shapes in different positions- moving them all up one fret at a time into a new key, and practising all the available triads in that key all over the guitar's neck. You will find it useful when doing this to locate the tonic triad and learn the triads above and below this point of reference. You will, quite quickly, become familiar with the symmetrical patterns that each key produces. Remember that every key has the same triad shapes in the same order and relationship to each other. The only difference is that they are found on different parts of the neck. Any triad that becomes inaccessible in a higher position can be found using the same shape an octave lower on the same group of strings, or by using an alternative shape on a different group of strings.

Once you have a key under your fingers, use it to create short improvisations in a similar manner to the examples given in Ex.19-20.

Chord Scales - Applying Triads

Before exploring some other types of chord scale, it would be useful to look at some ways of applying these first and second inversion triads. The examples given below are for solo guitar, although it is easy to adapt them for use in ensemble playing.[30] You should learn each exercise until you can play it fluently. I have not included a metronome speed because it is more important that you absorb the underlying principles rather than feeling that you have to treat them as technical studies.

Make sure that you use the suggested fingerings. Although it might be tempting to use alternatives, you will miss the whole point of the exercise if you fail to acquaint yourself with the underlying structure that these triads provide. Remember that these are strategies for improvisation. The objective is not to find the most convenient fingering with which to play an individual example as a finished piece of music, but to get the mind and fingers used to using chord scales as adaptable tools that can be applied effortlessly in numerous different ways, and in all sorts of different contexts.

You should also try to include other features, such as dynamics, different types of articulation (staccato, legato, etc.), graduation of volume (crescendos, diminuendos, etc.), tone colour and so on.

Ex.22 is a transcription of an improvised section taken from my piece 'New Shoes'. It alternates two bar phrases from the A Ionian mode, (or A Major scale) and D Dorian mode.

This passage consists of first and second inversion triads combined with scale tones. I have

---

30   See 'Solo and Ensemble Playing' chapter above.

bracketed and named each triad to enable you to easily distinguish between these important structural points of reference from the surrounding notes taken from the two modes.

You will notice that these chord tones are often played across the beat, starting at different parts of the bar and points within the phrase. This creates small fragments that combine with other chords and notes to form longer phrases. This is perhaps the most difficult aspect of using triadic material in a melodic way. If these triadic structures are placed too predictably, for example, one triad on each beat, or on every other beat, or on the same part of every beat; the results will tend to sound dull and unmusical.

Once the basic triad shapes have been learnt, your practice should focus on placing any of the three available notes, in any order, or combination, on any part of the bar, on any part of any beat within that bar, and at any point in the phrase. To do this you will have to develop the knack of accenting any of the three possible notes with the thumb, or any right hand finger. In my own playing I find myself relying a great deal on combinations of *p, i, m*. This is a technique adapted from banjo players by Chet Atkins, and since used by players like Lenny Breau and Ralph Towner. The following exercises are intended to give you some idea about how to practise and apply these techniques, but they can in no way exhaust the possibilities, which are almost endless. You should experiment with developing your own favourite patterns. Try using different finger combinations- they are all useful.

Ex.22.1 shows five triads- C (1st inversion), F (1st inversion), D min (root position), B dim (1st inversion) and F (2nd inversion). These triads are then used to form the following phrase. Make sure that you observe the indicated right and left hand fingerings, and that you accent the first semi quaver on each of the four beats.

This is difficult. You will instinctively want to accent only the notes played by the thumb.

A good way to practise this is to get used to playing the notes that make up the first beat, ending on the first note of beat two as follows:

When this feels comfortable, add the second beat, finishing on the accented note of beat three:

Now add beat three, finishing on the first note of beat four:

And finally ending on the first beat of the next bar to complete the phrase:

Ex.22.2 illustrates the same strategy as above, but this time with a descending, rather than an ascending phrase. It is based on a sequence of triads: F (second inversion), A min (root position) and C (first inversion).

I have again bracketed each individual triad shape to highlight the underlying structure. I suggest that you practise this phrase, and similar phrases of your own, in the same way as I outlined in Ex.22.1.

This approach feels very easy and natural to classical and fingerstyle players. It enables us to play rapid, complex melodic lines which can include large intervallic leaps that are much more difficult to achieve when using a plectrum.

By changing selected notes, you can suggest many different keys and modes using almost the same fingering. Once you can play Ex.22.2 fluently, and from memory, try the following variations:

a. Flatten the B naturals to B flats- changing the tonality of the original phrase from its present C Major, A Minor or F Lydian sound into F Major or D Natural Minor/D Aeolian mode.

b. If you take the original phrase, flatten the B to Bb, and change the C naturals to C sharp, you will imply a D harmonic Minor scale (or its third mode- F Ionian #5).

c. Raise the C naturals to C sharp to form a D melodic minor scale (or its third mode- F Lydian #5).

d. Taking the original phrase, flatten the E naturals to E flats. This will create a C Melodic Minor scale (or its fourth mode F Mixolydian #4)

e. Changing all of the F naturals to F sharps will create a phrase that could work well in the context of the keys of G Major or E minor (or G Major's seventh mode- F# Locrian).

f. Move the whole phrase up one fret to Db Major, Bb Minor (or Gb Lydian).

g. You can now make all of the same alterations in this new key, as you made for the key of the original phrase in C major.

h. Now try the same idea moving up one fret at a time until you have adapted Ex.22.2 to all twenty-four keys, and their corresponding modes.

Ex.22.3 uses the same left and right hand fingering as Ex.22.2, but this time I have simply started the phrase on a different part of the bar and moved all of the notes up one fret into the less familiar key of Db. Practising in this way is very useful for developing a more flexible approach, and avoids the very common error of placing each phrase in a predictable way, leading to creative stagnation and ruts.

Here is the same idea, returning to the original key, but starting on the last Semi-quaver, on the second beat, of the first bar.

The guitar is a difficult and complex instrument to learn. We have to get used to locating the same note in many different places, to co-ordinating the individual fingers of both the left *and* right hands to sound a single note, and so on. The ease with which we can take a collection of notes in one key, and move it into another, just by moving the same fingering up or down the neck is a welcome advantage which we should not hesitate to exploit.[31]

Pay particular attention when moving chords, intervals or phrases between the first and second positions, where the same pattern of notes will require an alternative fingering because of the unavailability of those handy open strings.

Ex.22.4 illustrates the equally important, but even more commonly overlooked principal of occasionally ending your phrases in varied and unexpected ways.

This is done by simply finishing the phrase earlier than intended, and is a lot more difficult to do than it sounds. When improvising, there is the ever-present danger of falling into what I might call 'automatic pilot'- a sort of auto-hypnotic state of mind in which we robotically reel off familiar patterns of notes that are already committed to 'finger memory', with no regard for the context of the music. Making a phrase shorter than intended, (or conversely adding notes and making it longer) obliges us to start the following phrase in a less predictable place and, in a similar way to the strategy described in Ex.22.3, keeps things fresh and interesting.

Ex.23 Triads can also be used to extend familiar chords, adding upper extensions and alterations. This exercise shows an improvisation based on a I, IV, V, I progression in the key of Ab Major.

The first two bars are built on the tonic Ab chord. I added a second inversion C min triad above the Ab root note, followed by Ab (root position), Eb (second inversion) and F min (first inversion) triads that collectively create the sound of a major 7th chord with an added 9th (and a major 6th on the last beat of the second bar).

---

31   Pianists, for example, - whose instrument affords them so many advantages in other areas, have to reconfigure their fingers to transpose the same phrase or chord when moving between keys.

The next two bars are built on the sub-dominant Db chord. Once again I have placed triads from the key of Ab Major over the Db root to create the sound of a very rich sounding Dbmaj7#11 chord. The G diminished triad (first inversion) on the first two beats of the third bar incorporates the #11th, 6th and root. The next triad is another F minor (this time in its second inversion) that contains the 5th, 3rd and major 7th, followed by another (first inversion) F minor triad in bar four.

Bars five and six outline an Eb dominant seventh chord, with a #9th and b9th as upper extensions. The first two beats of bar five consist of an Eb7 chord using only the root, third and seventh.[32] This is followed on beat three by a G diminished triad, which contains the 3rd, 5th and 7th. The following triad, on the first two beats of bar six, is a Gb (second inversion). The root of this triad is (enharmonically) the #9th of the Eb7 chord. The Db minor triad (first inversion), on the third beat of bar six contains Fb. This is the b9. (The final, Abmaj7 voicing could also be seen as a first inversion C min triad over an Ab root.)

The Gb and Db minor triads are played over the Eb7 chord to introduce more colourful, chromatically altered upper extensions over the basic dominant chord. The Gb triad is 'borrowed' from the key of Db Major (chord IV). This key is built on the subdominant of the tonic key of Ab Major. The Db minor triad is 'borrowed' from the key of Ab Minor (chord IV), which is the parallel minor of Ab Major.

When playing in a 'functional' harmonic setting (i.e. music that is based on traditional cadences made up of tonic, dominant, sub-dominant and secondary dominant chord relationships.), I try to follow two simple rules:

a. To prevent the occurrence of consecutive fourths and fifths I try to alternate different triad inversions.[33]
b. When playing tonic chords I avoid using triads that contain the IVth. (In the key of C this would be F) In a similar way I avoid using the tonic note when playing a dominant seventh chord (unless they are used as passing notes). This is because they are dissonant and undermine the functional nature of these specific chords.[34]

---

32   This voicing is commonly used in Jazz and is often called a 'shell' chord. It contains the essential elements of a seventh chord, without the clutter of the fifth. It is easy to grab, can be readily adapted to form other types of seventh chord, It is also easy to add other notes, to create 9th, 11th and 13th chords- or their alterations.

33   Consecutive fourths and fifths are considered 'weak' in traditional, functional harmonic writing. This is not the case in modal harmony and more contemporary composition. (See 'Contemporary Harmony- Romanticism through The Twelve Tone Row' by Ludmila Ulehla.)

34   Once again, this is applicable to traditional, functional harmony, and less so in more contemporary music.

Ex23.1 Using closely related keys, as a source of chromatic notes and chords that are 'outside' of the home key is a very useful strategy. You should memorise the following two rules for the keys of C Major/Minor and then practice applying the same idea in the remaining twenty-two keys.

    a. In a major key, you can borrow triads from its dominant, or subdominant major, and minor keys, and from its parallel minor key. In the key of C Major, for example, you can borrow triads from- F Major/Minor, G Major/Minor or C Minor.

The following table shows the chromatic triads that are available in the key of C Major. Triads derived from minor keys are taken from the Natural, Harmonic and Melodic Minor scales.[35]

Chromatic Triad.	Triads relationship to the key of C Major.	Key(s) from which triad was 'borrowed'.
Cm	Im	C Minor, F Minor, G Minor.
Db	bII	F Minor
Ddim	IIdim	C Minor, F Minor.
D	II	G Major, G Minor.
Eb	bIII	C Minor, F minor, G Minor.
Eb#5	BIII#5	C Minor
Edim	IIIdim	F Major, F Minor, G Minor.
Fm	IVm	C Minor, F Minor.
F#dim	#IVdim	G Minor.
Gdim	Vdim	F Minor
Gm	Vm	C Minor, F Major, F Minor.
Ab	bVI	C Minor, F Minor.
Ab#5	BVI#5	F Minor.
Adim	VIdim	C Minor, G Minor.
Bbm	bVIIm	F Minor
Bb	bVII	C Minor, F Major, F Minor.
Bb#5	bVII#5	G Minor.
Bm	VIIm	G Major.

    b. In a minor key, you can borrow a chord from its dominant and subdominant minor keys. In the key of C Minor, therefore you can 'borrow' triads from the keys of F Minor and G Minor. (Natural, Harmonic and Melodic.)

---

35   See Ex.7.

The following table shows the available chromatic triads in the key of C Minor.

Chromatic Triad.	Triads relationship to the key of C Minor.	Key(s) from which triad was 'borrowed'.
(C)	(Imaj)	F Minor, G Minor.
Db	bIImaj	F Minor.
D	IImaj	G Minor.
Eb	bIII	F Minor, G Minor.
(Edim)	(IIIdim)	F Minor.
F#dim	#IVdim	G Minor.
Gdim	Vdim	F Minor.
Gm	Vm	G Minor.
(Ab#5)	(bVI#5)	F Minor.
Adim	VIdim	G Minor, F Minor.
Bbm	bVIIm	F Minor.
Bb#5	bV	G Minor.

The bracketed C, Edim and Ab#5 triads all contain the E natural, which is the major third of C Minor. They should, therefore, be treated with some caution as they disturb the minor tonality. These chords, if used at all, should only function as passing chords. (The C triad, when it is used as the final chord in the minor key, is the so called 'Tierce de Picardie')

It can be helpful, when getting used to using chromatic triads in this way, to take a very simple and familiar chord sequence and experiment with different triad combinations over the dominant V chord, keeping everything else the same.

Ex.23.2 is based on a II, V, I progression in the key of A Major. This conveniently allows us to play the roots of both the tonic and dominant chords on the fifth and sixth strings, giving us plenty of freedom to experiment with these sounds without having to worry about awkward fingerings. It can be played with either straight or swung quavers.

Insert the following alternatives into bar two of Ex.23.2. I have shown each variation firstly in the form of block chords, followed by the same idea played as an arpeggio.

Now try improvising your own 'fills'. Pay attention to the melody. Make sure that you connect the final E in bar one to the C# in bar three in a logical way. There is no need to use purely borrowed triads from neighbouring keys. These can be combined with diatonic triads from A Major.

Although chord roots are important when playing without a bass player, they don't need to be included all of the time. Like a good piece of orchestral music, your improvisation needs lots of textural variety that should range from a single voice through to rich, multiple voiced chords and counterpoint. When you do include chord roots don't feel that you must always make them last for the whole bar. (Revise the chapter on bass lines and counterpoint.) Often the demands of left hand fingering make this impossible anyway. You should also practice placing them on different parts of the bar, avoiding too much repetition - which quickly becomes predictable and boring.

The examples given here are deliberately simple to read and play, as my intention is to convey the underlying concept, rather than have you spend hours puzzling over complex transcriptions. Clearly, it is essential to practice similar ideas in all twenty-four major and minor keys, in all positions. Pace yourself! This will take a lifetime but it is worth the effort. Being less familiar with the more remote keys doesn't prevent you from playing great music, it does, however limit you.

All instruments have keys that sound better, and that are easier to play in. The guitar is no different. Jazz guitarists have to get used to playing in flat keys. This is because the traditional 'front line' instruments (saxophone and trumpet) are in their comfort zone when there are flats in the key signature. The guitar, as a humble 'rhythm section' instrument finds itself playing almost permanently in keys in which its natural resonance and timbre are repressed.[36] The advantage of this is that Jazz players learn very quickly how to get the best out of these keys.

Contemporary Jazz and Improvised Music tends to be more democratic in that it allows all instruments in an ensemble more equal status. This has radically altered the possibilities of the music and consequently placed a whole spectrum of new demands on musicians.

---

36   I sometimes think that when playing in this setting it would be to the guitarist's advantage to re-tune the guitar a semitone higher and transpose the parts accordingly.

As noted in Ex.23 (rule b.), when playing in a 'functional' harmonic setting there are certain 'avoid' notes that are normally regarded as dissonant when played against specific chords. In Modal music, this is not the case. Instead, we can regard all of the notes available to us in any mode as potentially useful, both melodically and harmonically. There are, however notes that define the sound of a particular mode and are particularly useful. They are the notes that distinguish one particular mode from another.

For example, in the Dorian mode the (major) sixth is important because the other three modes, derived from the major scale, that contain the minor third (Aeolian, Phrygian and Locrian) all contain a minor sixth. In the Phrygian mode, it is the combination of the minor sixth, the perfect fifth, and minor second, that distinguish it. In the Lydian mode, it is the augmented fourth and major seventh, and so on. When combined with the root and major or minor third these 'colour' notes define the distinctive sound and emotional territory that each mode can offer.

You may have noticed that these colour notes are always taken from the two minor second steps that are found within the scales structure. In C Major/ Ionian, for example these would be the III and IV, (E and F) and the VII and I, (B and C). In D Dorian, the same two groups of notes are found on the II and III and the VI and VII degrees, in the Phrygian they are on the I and II and V and VI, and so on.

If we investigate the Melodic and Harmonic Minor scales and their corresponding modes, we find that there are three minor second steps in the structure of the Harmonic Minor (between the II - III, V - VI and the VII - I) and two contained in the Melodic Minor (between the II - III, and VII - I).

This opens up some fascinating possibilities for chords that are not constructed using the principal of stacking thirds (or fourths). However, as we are presently investigating the use of triads, we will explore some of these ideas later on.

When we are improvising an accompanying part with others our role is to support and interact with them, choosing chords, intervals and lines that define the prevailing harmony without getting in the way or cluttering things up. When playing in a modal context combining triads with the mode's root is an excellent way to do this. It allows us too more precisely control the different note combinations and durations than if we only rely on larger fixed chord voicings. When playing with a bass player, we can often abandon even the root note and concentrate only on the upper notes of the chord.

Ex.24 illustrates the use of triads to create the impression of larger, more complex chords in a modal context. I have chosen a Bb Dorian mode to show how I might apply this idea in a situation where I don't have the luxury of an open string root. Play this example at around 80 bpm so that you can hear the way the superimposed triads above the Bb root create the impression of a Bbm chord with added 7ths, 9ths, 11ths, and 13ths.

Bear in mind that these triads are presented here in a deliberately simple way. Once you can play this example smoothly, you should use the right hand fingers to extract different intervallic combinations from these basic triad shapes. Try introducing rhythms that are more varied by playing these chords and intervals at different points in the bar, creating interesting accents that drive the music forward.

Triads are also useful when playing atonally. They offer convenient, consistent shapes that can be played in symmetrical and asymmetrical patterns. These provide recognisable structure, without the need to become pinned down by explicit diatonic or modal references. When played using open voicings, (see below) they facilitate the use of the wider intervals that play such an important role in atonal music.

Some improvising musicians choose to play entirely within an atonal[37]

framework. This demands just as much skill, focus, and discipline as any other approach to music making. I am often surprised, and a little saddened, to hear the same sort of insults and innuendoes that were directed towards the pioneers of Free Jazz sixty years ago, still being repeated today.

It is an unfortunate and almost inevitable human trait that we should tend to polarise ourselves between two apparently opposing points of view. For my own part, I prefer to regard atonal music as part of the same spectrum of available sounds as tonal music. When I am improvising or composing, I feel that I am telling a sort of musical story. This story unfolds in its own logical way, with each phrase or section leading on to the next. I often find that atonal sections naturally grow out of tonal ones (and visa versa). This seems to happen as a consequence of the music's evolving momentum, when its established boundaries begin to 'loosen' and the music itself seems to demand a further range of expressive possibilities.

Ex.25 for example, shows an atonal passage of music, which is created using only second inversion major triads. These are played entirely on the second, third, and fourth strings. Use the right hand fingers in a similar way to that outlined in Ex.22. My left hand fingering when playing this passage consisted almost exclusively of first and third finger partial barres.

---

37   I am using the word 'tonal' here, in its strict sense. Many musicians, who are commonly regarded as 'atonal' in their approach, seem to have created what we could regard as their own unique 'tonality'. This is easily recognisable and consistently and rigorously applied.

So far, I have only shown how to use these triads in closed position, and either as arpeggios or block chords. There are of course plenty of other alternatives.

A closed triad can be opened up by raising or lowering one or more of its voices by an octave.

Ex.26 illustrates some of the possible voicings that can be derived from first and second inversion major triads. I have, in each case, taken the middle voice and either raised or lowered it by one octave. The tablature notation suggests only one fingering for each chord. In contrast the standard notation on the stave can be interpreted in a much more flexible way.

Learn each shape as a major triad, and then change it into minor, diminished, and augmented triads, by raising or lowering the third or root as appropriate.

Now go back and review Ex's. 21 to 25 choosing one or two open position triads, and creating your own versions of each exercise with this new sound.

Moving one, or more of its voices, up or down a chosen scale, can also extend closed, or open position triads.

Ex.27 is intended to outline the possibilities of this strategy in a rudimentary way. I have taken a first inversion, tonic triad in the key of Bb and extended one or two of its voices into melodic lines.

Don't worry too much about sustaining all of the written note lengths to their full value. As in all guitar music, we have to allow ourselves a certain degree of freedom in this regard. Because of the physical limitations of fingering notes in different positions on the guitars neck, note lengths are sometimes best regarded as suggestive, or aspirational rather than physically possible.

In a similar way, we are also at liberty to sustain notes of a shorter written duration. Whether unavoidable or deliberate this apparent limitation can produce some beautiful 'accidents' that are one of the glories of the instrument. Once again we can see, in this context, how the standard treble clef notation is more useful than tablature because of the way in which it can suggest alternative fingering possibilities.

Clearly, these strategies are useful when experimenting with the contrapuntal ideas that are outlined in the 'Bass Lines And Cantus Firmi' chapter above.

As before, you should apply this idea in as many different ways as you can, using different chords, inversions, voicings, major and minor keys, modes and so on. The possibilities of this approach are vast, and would require another book to do them justice. Try to make this, and all of the other strategies in this book your own. Take each exercise and adapt it to your own tastes and musical vision. All of us are unique individuals, and one of the reasons I love improvised music so much, is because of the way in which this individuality can find expression.

Fourth Chords

Chords built up from stacked fourths, rather than thirds, are another fantastic resource. From a guitarist's point of view they are easy to visualise and finger and can be used as a gateway out of purely diatonic sounds into a more open tonality. Fourth chords also sound good when mixed together with more conventional chords built in thirds, as well as other more complex voicings, and can provide a useful platform on which to build melodic ideas.

Ex.28 shows ascending four note fourth chords in the keys of C Major and C (Melodic and Harmonic) Minor.

Fourth Chords- C Major.

Strings one to four.

Strings two to five.

Strings four to six.

Fourth Chords- C (Harmonic) Minor.
Strings one to four.

Strings two to five.

Strings three to six.

Fourth Chords- C (Melodic) Minor.
Strings one to four.

Strings two to five.[38]

---

38   The first chord in this sequence is often described as a B7#9. This is a very familiar shape to Jazz, Rock and Blues guitarists who usually describe it as an altered dominant chord that is built up in thirds, with the fifth omitted. This can now be seen in its proper context, as a four note fourth chord.

If we build a chord in thirds from the leading note of a C Melodic Minor scale, we get a Bm7b5. To my ear the seventh mode of the C Melodic Minor scale works for both of these chords, but does note work for the so-called B7 'altered' chord with its implied b9, #9, b5, and #5. (See 'Chord/ Scale

Relationships- Limitations' chapter above.)

Strings three to six.

This gives us eight different types of chord, built on combinations of perfect, augmented and diminished fourths.

Ex.29 illustrates these eight chord types built on a C root.

Most of these structures can be seen as partial 11th chords with no fifths. The chord in bar five can be seen as a Cm7b5, and in the eighth bar as C7b5.

These chords can easily be converted into triads by omitting the top or bottom note, or into larger five and six note chords by adding more fourths above and below. Out of all of these possibilities, I generally find the three-note triad form of the fourth chord to be the most useful, however it is important to be able to visualise these chords all over the neck so you should learn them in groups of three, four, five and six strings.

If the notes of these chords are re-ordered, we get some interesting and familiar chords. For example, the three note fourth structure C, F, Bb, (Csus4) can become an Bbsus2 (F, Bb, C). These same notes when stacked up in reverse order (Bb, F, C) form a chord made up of perfect fifths stacked on top of a Bb root.

Understanding the way in which these different chord structures inter-relate enables us to maximise the guitar's potential for varied and colourful chord voicings and arpeggios. It can also help us to avoid the constant danger of getting ourselves into musical ruts through the over use of more familiar fingerings.

Ex.30 like Ex.18 is based on the opening bars of the Bill Evans ballad 'Turn Out The Stars', and illustrates the way in which you can replace some of the familiar written chords, with those built up in fourths. (You might find it useful, once you are used to working with the ideas in this chapter, to experiment with combining these different strategies.)

I have placed brackets around the areas where I have replaced the written chords with fourth chords, and have again, for the sake of clarity, limited myself to block chords. This example can become much more complex if you exploit the intervallic and melodic possibilities inherent within these voicings. (See 'Chord Scales- Applying Triads' chapter above.)

The bracketed fourth chords in the second bar are borrowed from the key of D Minor. (The sub-dominant key, of the tonic A Minor.) Those in the third bar combine voicings from the tonic A Natural and Harmonic Minor scales. The fourth triads in bars five and six are all derived from the key of Eb Major.

Fourth chords have a distinctive quality that enables them to sound consonant with each other, even when they contain notes that lie outside of a specific mode or key. 'Impressionist' composers such as Debussy and Ravel re-discovered their inherent beauty after they had been out of fashion in European music since the Middle Ages[39]. McCoy Tyner is often credited with introducing them into Jazz as a solution to the demands of the modal and free innovations introduced by John Coltrane.

Ex.31 contrasts three different harmonisations of a simple melody in the E Phrygian Mode. The first version uses only diatonic chords made up of parallel perfect and augmented fourths.

---

39   The earliest written record we have of this approach to polyphony is found in Musica Enchiriadis, written around 900AD. Ludmila Ulehla in her excellent 'Contemporary Harmony, Romanticism through the Twelve-Tone Row' gives a detailed account of the use of fourth (and fifth) chords from the early twentieth centaury onwards.

Because of the rigid application of these diatonic, parallel intervals, this version tends to sound a little awkward and dull. However, as I have demonstrated in earlier exercises' these large block chords can be broken up into smaller units, arpeggiated, or added to in other ways. This adds rhythmic, melodic and harmonic movement that can make the music come alive.

Using parallel intervals in this way is a very useful strategy for the improvising guitarist. Because of the nature of the instrument, these intervals are easy to find. They allow us to instantly harmonise an improvised melody. They also enable us to accompany another musician, without dictating the direction of their improvisation by choosing unexpected and unwelcome chords that suggest, for example, an inappropriate dominant or tonic function. This is because superimposed fourths avoid the tonal implications of leading notes that are such a central element in the tertiary triads, and seventh chords of functional harmony.

The second version follows the same melody, but this time harmonises it by consistently adding two perfect fourth intervals below each note. This approach creates chords that no longer strictly conform to the prevailing key, but which, never the less, because of their symmetrical construction, have a satisfying sound and logic all of their own.

This approach produces a much more contemporary, 'edgy' sound. It is useful when accompanying others because it tends to prompt the soloist towards more chromatic freedom. It is also useful when playing solo, functioning as a bridge between tonal passages into more chromatic territory

In the third example I have inverted the notes of some of the chords to create sus2 voicings and chords made up of stacked fifth intervals. (See Ex.30 above) This, to my ear produces a very full and satisfying sound reminiscent of Ralph Vaughan Williams or John Taverner. The combination of chords introduces more variety, and varying the chords voicings creates more contrapuntal movement between the parts.

The bass lines, in all three examples, are mostly constructed from notes taken from the upper triad, which are then doubled an octave below, or by adding an additional fourth note to the triad, using an appropriate interval. I have also, on occasion added notes to the bass line that are not derived from these fourth chord structures to preserve its melodic continuity.

Ex.32 Fourth chords do not necessarily have to be related to a key or mode. If we superimpose perfect fourths over a chosen root, we create a chord that is consonant in its lower parts but which becomes successively more remote from the overtone series as successive notes are added.

This example builds the chord from an E root; however, you can start with any note. Each one will contain the same twelve notes, but will sound unique because of the way in which they are ordered.

This large chord can be broken down into smaller units, or constructed with some of its notes left out. The chosen notes can then be re-ordered, moving them up or down an octave to create beautiful clusters[40]. Selecting notes that are either closer or more distant from the root can control the degree of consonance or dissonance.

---

40   Chords that contain minor and major second intervals, usually in conjunction with thirds, fourths, fifths etc.

I suggest that you spend some time experimenting with these ideas. If you find a chord that you like, write it down in your own chord dictionary. Once you have digested their sound and physical shape, they will become an integral part of your own style and can become valuable springboards to new improvisational ideas and compositions.

For the sake of clarity, I have shown each of these approaches separately. However, you should bear in mind that they often sound best when they are combined. Try to avoid using a single technique for too long. Pianists and guitarists, for example, when working with Miles Davis often used three note fourth chords alternating with second inversion triads. The top note of these chords usually followed the prevailing scale, often over a pedal bass, or repeated bass riff. This approach would often be used in conjunction with other types of chords and chord connections within the same piece of music.

Composers such as Bela Bartok, Charles Ives and Igor Stravinsky, used similar strategies, as do many contemporary composers and improvisers. The wealth and variety of music that can be produced from a simple idea is a testimony to the individual creativity of these musicians, as well as the expressive power of the musical language that we have inherited from them.

Exploiting A Chord's Melodic Potential

One of the things that I find most appealing about using my right hand fingers, rather than a plectrum, is the way in which I can easily extract melodies from chords, whilst retaining a sense of the underlying harmony. This is obviously of critical importance when playing solo, but is also of great value in other contexts as well.

Different chords offer different possibilities. Larger chords offer greater melodic choice within their structure, whilst smaller chords are more flexible in their application.

Obviously, triads tend to be quite limited in their potential to extract interesting melodic patterns from, because they offer only a narrow choice of notes and intervals. This range of options is increased when a fourth note is added, and dramatically increased with the addition of further extensions.

It is also interesting to note the way in which the size of a chord determines the range of possible applications for that chord. A Bb major triad, for example, can be located within three Major scales, two Harmonic Minor scales, two Melodic Minor scales, and four diminished scales. A total of eleven possible scales and forty-nine associated modes. If we add an A to this triad, turning it into a Bbmaj7 or a Bb/A we limit its possible applications to two Major and one Harmonic Minor scale. The addition of the #11 (E) limits it further to only one Major and one Harmonic Minor scale, and their associated modes.

I find it very useful to think about chords in this way. When I first started to study Jazz and improvised music, my teachers convinced me that I had to use only chords that included 7ths, 9ths 11ths and 13ths and so on. I dutifully spent my days incorporating only these familiar 'Jazz guitar chord shapes' into my playing, ignoring the value of smaller, simpler chords. This effort certainly wasn't wasted, as these chords continue to be an important element in my music. However, experience, and my own research into the music of other improvising musicians has led me to the conviction that it is far too limiting for us to restrict ourselves to any one catch all solution.

My study of the improvisations of Jazz pianists in particular, revealed the way in which they often vary their harmonies by using the whole spectrum of different chord types. The books by George Van Eps and Mick Goodrick also provided me with some new perspectives, adapting many strategies used by these same pianists to the guitar.

Many contemporary Jazz guitarists, in contrast to their predecessors, often use simple triads and open fifth intervals in combination with other types of chord. Bill Frisell in a recent interview commented on how, during the recording of Kenny Wheeler's beautiful 'Angel Song' (ECM), he had simplified many of the very complex chords that Kenny had originally written out for him, so as to allow himself more melodic freedom. On other occasions, Bill can be heard creating massive, complex chord structures, often using loop and delay effects to extend the guitars physical limitations. This flexibility towards different harmonic approaches is a hallmark of contemporary Jazz and Improvised Music. It is reflected in an openness towards all aspects of music that I find inspiring.

I have dealt with the application of simpler three and four note chords in some detail in preceding chapters. I would now like to spend some time outlining my approach to using larger, more complex structures.

Ex.33 shows how I might exploit the inherent melodic possibilities within a sequence of larger, more complex chords. Familiarise yourself with the following melody;

Now play through these chords, taking note of the fact that they contain all of the notes of the melody (except for the C# in the second bar).

Finally combine both of these elements. Articulate the melody by subtly accenting its constituent notes with the appropriate right hand fingers, keeping the underlying arpeggio notes slightly softer.

Improvising, or composing in this way requires the combination of several different skills. These larger chords often require big left hand stretches and sustained barre chords. The right hand needs to be able to freely accent specific notes with different fingers, (in a similar way to exercises 22 to 22.4), and to be able to develop rhythmic motives that can combine with the available notes to build coherent melodies. It is also essential, when required, to effectively dampen unwanted notes from ringing over, ensuring a strong clean rhythmic feel.

Ex.34 is taken from the closing bars of my piece 'For I.S'. It consists of descending, rapidly repeated first inversion triad arpeggios. These notes should be left to ring for as long as possible.

The simple melody, introduced in the second section, is played with the ring finger. This is a good exercise for developing independence of the right hand fingers, and to practise highlighting a melody over a quieter underlying accompanying part. The melody does not have to be placed on the third beat of each bar, as I have written here. You might like to experiment by placing it on the first, second or fourth beats.

Bearing in mind the old adage, that 'there is nothing new under the sun', I recommend Mauro Giuliani's one hundred and twenty exercises for the right hand as a useful way of developing the necessary independence and strength in the fingers. This is a standard text for Classical Guitarists that is readily adaptable to our needs as improvisers, although you may wish to vary the chords in these studies, as they are rather limited.

If you are able to track a copy down, (as it has sadly long been out of print) Ralph Towner's book 'Improvisation and Performance Techniques for Classical and Acoustic Guitar' offers invaluable guidance on this and many other topics.

Whilst I am on the subject, there are also obvious technical, theoretical, and artistic advantages in playing and studying the entire Classical Guitar repertoire. The accumulated wisdom and insight contained in this material is easily adapted to our own needs, and the effort required to familiarise ourselves with it is repaid a thousand fold.

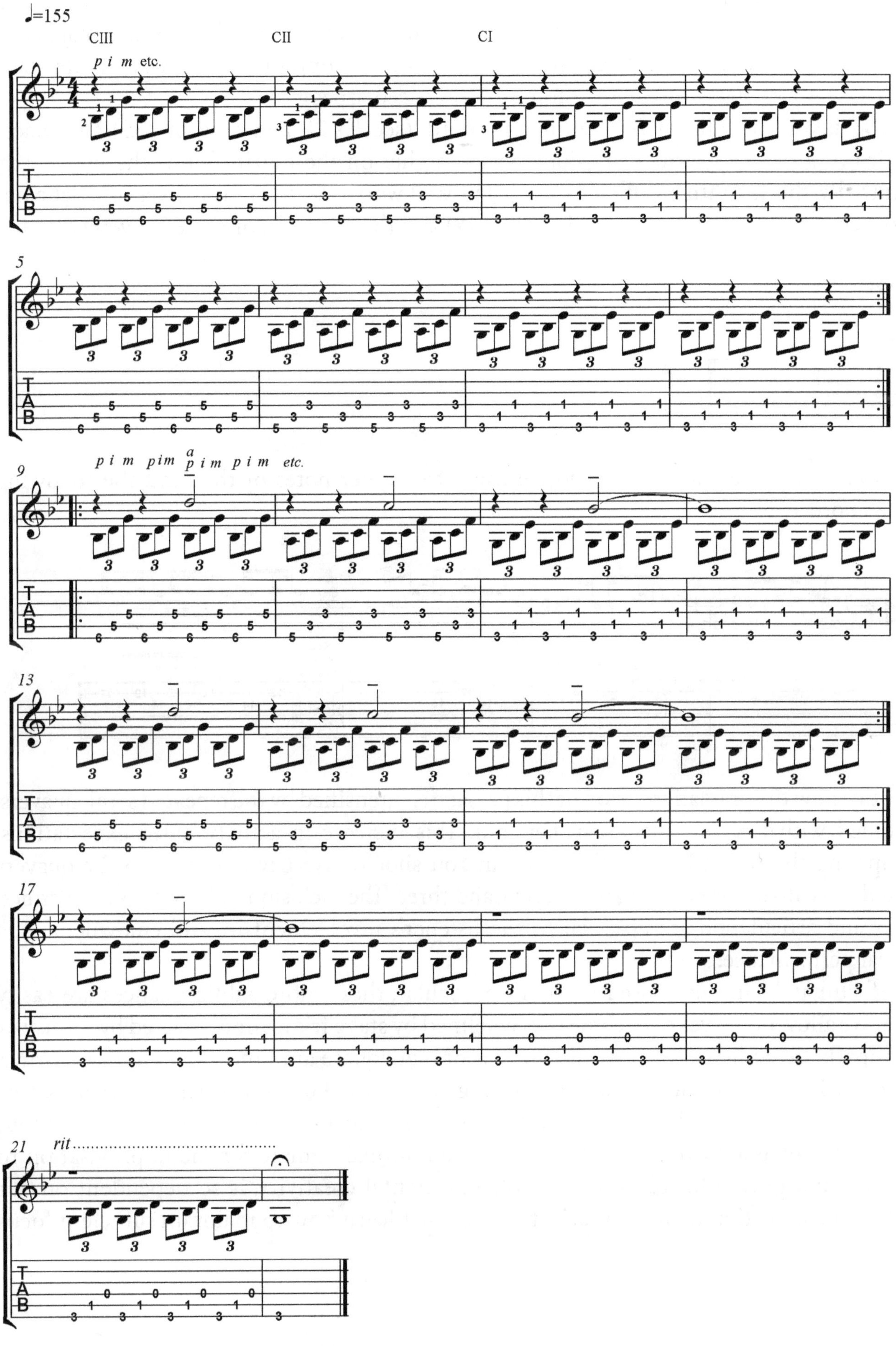
♩=155
CIII
CII
CI
p i m etc.
p i m pim a p i m p i m etc.
rit.

Clearly, the way in which we voice the chords is important here. I often find it helpful to combine the notes of a given chord, at least in part, into clusters. This locates major and minor second intervals on adjacent strings, giving me the opportunity to incorporate short scale like patterns, rather than just more widely spaced arpeggios.

Ex.35 takes a familiar 'E7#9' dominant chord, (see Ex.28 and footnote 35) and places its third (G# on the fourth string) one octave higher on the fourth fret of the first string. Admittedly, this is a rather difficult stretch, but well worth the effort as it gives us a delicious minor second clash between the major 3rd (G#) and the #9th (Fx, or more conveniently, G).

I have now created a melodic motive using the upper notes of this, and the following Asus2 chord.

Notice how the dramatic tension of this passage is intensified by the repeated semi-quavers, combined with the diminuendo in bar four. This increase in activity raises expectations, anticipating the repeat back to the first bar. You should also pay attention to the quavers marked staccato at the end of bars one, two, and three. The inclusion of factors like dynamics, colour and articulation are essential to the listener's involvement in, and enjoyment of, a musical performance.

Unfortunately, in improvised music in particular, these more subtle nuances are easily lost. If we allow ourselves to become overwhelmed by stage fright, or distracted by a noisy or unsympathetic audience, or if we are victims of inadequate amplification and monitoring, we can easily fall into the trap of 'just playing the notes'. For improvising musicians, this situation is a disaster. This is because we are so reliant upon these subtleties. Without them we are unable to generate the necessary emotional climate for the improvisation to take root and grow. Our physical control, and mental creativity, is so dependent on our emotional connection with the music, that we must learn how to maintain sufficient focus to enable us to disregard all environmental distractions and stay connected only with the music.[41]

Ex.36 is a short section from my piece, 'Catch And Fall'. It is a good example of the way in which I extract melody notes from the surrounding chord arpeggios by accenting specific notes with my right hand fingers. (Watch out for the 'Hinged Barre' in bars five and six.)

You may also have noticed the way in which I have combined the fourth chords (over an A pedal) in the seventh and eighth bars, with other types of chord. When placed above an A pedal (ostinato or ground bass) these create an 'A dominant' sound that eventually leads to the key of D Minor. The rhythmic figure played by the thumb on the open A string allows more freedom for the left hand to play scale-based ideas above it. These contrast nicely with the richer chords and accented arpeggios in the preceding bars, keeping the music varied and interesting.

---

41   For the majority of musicians this skill is hard won. Only repeated exposure to different circumstances and types of audience can acclimatise us to the realities of performing. We gradually learn to develop a mental toughness and self-awareness that identifies and insulates us from destructive habits of thought whilst we are performing.

This is why I encourage all of my students, at every level, to actively seek out opportunities to perform. These might include playing to friends and family, taking regular guitar lessons, attending a college or university course, taking graded examinations, taking part in local amateur music events, playing with others, becoming an active member of a guitar society or club (or starting their own). Even the simple act of regularly recording and listening to your self can be of great value in preparing for a live audience or recording studio.

Those who aspire to become professional players and teachers should also be prepared to play in cover bands, and look for other commercial playing opportunities. The music may not be to your taste, but the experience is invaluable. It is better than working at the local supermarket, and often provides new opportunities to meet and work with other accomplished musicians, with similar interests and motives to your own.

Although I tend to regard the first six bars of this passage as a fixed, pre-composed part of this piece. I realised, when I came to transcribe it, the extent to which I varied it with each successive performance. I often find myself altering the melody, and even altering the time signature of individual bars, to create a less symmetrical, more edgy feel. This highlights an important distinction between the way in which I would interpret a written score, when teaching a classical guitar piece, and the way in which I approach my own and other peoples music, as an improviser.

I remember an interviewer, on BBC Radio Four, asking Jan Garbarek to estimate the proportion of his groups music that was pre-arranged, as opposed to improvised. He immediately replied that they improvised all of the time. The interviewer was clearly surprised by this; assuming that she was hearing alternating composed and improvised sections. This is an understandable mistake, because some parts of the live performances do sound similar to the studio recordings. Closer examination of Jan's music, at concerts and on live recordings, reveals that his group (along with many other improvising musicians), are playing an agreed, recognisable theme, that is re interpreted each time it is performed. These themes are usually interspersed with improvised sections, based on chord sequences, melodic and rhythmic motives, as well as completely free, spontaneous parts.

My understanding of these issues has, over the years, become much more nuanced. Indian Sitarist Partha Bose, during a memorable conversation late one evening, explained to me how musicians from his own classical tradition are equally flexible in their approach to combining the 'composed' sections of a Raga with other, less structured elements. Graham Collier, in his wonderful book 'The Jazz Composer- Moving The Music Off The Paper' explains, in some detail, similar approaches in the music of Duke Ellington and others.

Ex.37. The use of different voicings and chord inversions can greatly expand our melodic choices when improvising. I often find it helpful, when thinking about extending a section of a piece through improvisation, to visualise two or three alternative ways of playing the same chord progression. I might choose, for example, to go from lower pitched voicings to higher ones, or higher to lower. Chosen chords might incorporate combinations of open and fretted notes, Barres, widely spaced intervals, or notes clustered together, (as in Ex.35). All of these choices will have a direct bearing on the melodic possibilities that are available to us.

The use of 'slash' chords is another convenient way to invert familiar chords. We might decide, for example, to play D/C as an alternative to D7, Em/D as an alternative to Em7, or G/E for Em9.

CAGED chord shapes can be systematically inverted by simply raising each note, on each string, to the next highest chord tone.

This example shows a first position D7 chord that has been inverted by raising the root (D), on the open fourth string, to the third (F#) on the fourth fret of the same string. The Fifth (A), on the third string, is raised to the seventh (C) on the fifth fret of the same string, and so on.

Here is the same 'D shape', chord with the third and fifth flattened, turning it into a Dm7b5. This has also been moved vertically up the same group of four strings, in the same way. (You might have noticed the sixth position Abm6 chord, as well as the Fm/D, and Ddim/C slash chords.)

This example shows the same idea, applied to an 'A shape', Bbmaj7. (These voicings also contain two slash chords; Dm/Bb, and Bb/A.)

I recommend that you spend some time acquainting yourself with all of the possible inversions for all of the common chord types[42], using all of the five CAGED shapes. You will find that some of these shapes are more practical than others. Rather than try to use them all at once, you should choose those that most easily lie beneath the fingers, and focus on incorporating these into your playing. You can always try using some of the more exotic ones later.

It is also worth noting that shapes that might prove to be impractical as harmonic arpeggios or chords can prove to be useful as melodic arpeggio patterns.[43]

Ex.38 shows another extract from 'Graceful Dream' (See also Ex.1 - 3). Play through the chords a few times. Now play the melody over these chords, noting the close relationship between the chord shape and the melodic outline. Once you have got used to my version, you might like to experiment with your own variations, based on the same idea.

---

42   Maj7, dom7, m7, m7b5, dim7, etc.

43   The notes of harmonic arpeggios are sustained, ringing over one another. Melodic arpeggios, on the other hand, contain notes that are played one at a time.

You can see that the uppermost note in each chord gradually descends in the first three bars before beginning to ascend again in bars four and five. This forms a smooth melodic contour that gives shape to the melody that follows.

I have called the fourth chord in this sequence an E9b6/G# or G#7#5. This is an interesting example of the way in which dominant 7th chords with a raised 5th can be raised or lowered by major thirds, without altering their function.

The E9b6/G# is of course an inversion of the dominant 7th chord of A Minor. In this case, the fifth of the chord (B) is omitted, but still implied. The b6, or b13, (C) is regarded as an upper extension to the basic E7 chord.[44] We could also choose to regard this same chord as a G#7#5, visualising it as the 'Altered Dominant' chord that can be enharmonically built on the seventh degree of the A Melodic Minor scale, or a G#7b13, built on the fifth degree of the C# Melodic Minor scale.

Raising this same chord shape a major third by moving its root from G#, up to B# (or C) on the eighth fret of the sixth string, gives us a C7#5 (or B#7#5) chord.

Enharmonically this chord, again, contains the root (E), third (G#), and b6 (C) of the original E7 chord along with an additional #11 (A# or, enharmonically speaking; Bb). This same chord is also often regarded as being a B#7#5, built on the seventh degree of a C# Melodic Minor scale, or a C7b13, which is found on the fifth degree of the F Melodic or Harmonic Minor scale.

---

44   See also, 'Chord / Scale Relationships- Limitations', chapter above.

Raising this chord up another major third brings it up to a root position E7b6 (or b13), this time without the 9th.

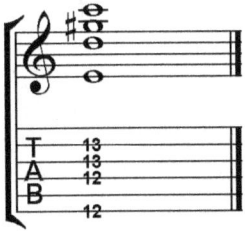

This could also imply an E7#5 built on the seventh degree of the F Melodic Minor scale, or as an inversion of any of the other chords above!

There are obvious advantages in acquainting ourselves with this type of multiple application, whether playing solo, improvising a melody, or accompanying others. The symmetry of these chord voicings gives us the opportunity to easily introduce chromatic notes into a key. They offer numerous alternatives with which to re shape the melodic contour, and vary the harmonic direction and texture.

Similar relationships exist between 7b5, and 7#11 chords. These can, like the 7#5 chord, be raised or lowered by major thirds without changing the chords function.

The 7b9 and diminished 7th chords have similar properties. It is common practice to invert a 7b9 chord by building a diminished 7th chord on either its 3rd, 5th, 7th or b9th.[45] This yields an easily applied pattern ascending or descending minor thirds.

We can leave tonality even further behind, whilst retaining these familiar chord shapes, by using the whole tone and diminished scales.[46] These are both scales that, because of their symmetrical construction, have a coherent, logical sound, but which do not fit into any key. The whole tone scale contains, (amongst many other possibilities) six 7b5 and six 7#5 chords, each one built on a scale tone. The Diminished Scale contains (amongst many other possibilities) eight dim7 chords, four 7b5 chords four 7b9 chords, and four 7#9 chords. European composers began exploiting these resources towards the end of the nineteenth century, and were followed a few decades later by American songwriters and Jazz musicians.

The use of these materials is exhaustively detailed in many books on Jazz and Classical theory. If you haven't done so already, I would encourage you to spend some time studying and learning to apply these ideas. I would also feel it is important to stress the value of learning from Classical scores, and from (preferably your own) transcriptions of Jazz, and other improvised performances.

Both Jazz and Classical music have developed their own language to describe harmony. The 'Italian' sixth of classical harmony becomes the tri- tone, or b5 substitute in Jazz. Classical musicians describe chords in terms of a figured bass, whilst Jazz, and other musicians have developed the use of chord symbols, and so on.

---

45   For example, try using an Ab, B, D, orFdim7 chord instead of a G7, or its tri-tone substitute Db7.

46   The Diminished Scale can be constructed by taking two diminished seventh arpeggios a tone apart, and then laying them out in scale order. For example, a Cdim7 contains the notes C, Eb, Gb, and Bbb. Ddim7 is made up of D, F, Ab, and Cb. This, (using enharmonic equivalents) gives us the C diminished scale; C D Eb F Gb Ab A B C. The same type of structure, consisting of alternating tones and semitones, can also be arrived at by combining a Cdim7 with a Dbdim7.

The Whole Tone Scale is a six-note scale that divides the octave equally into six whole tones. For example, the C Whole Tone Scale would consist of the notes C D E F# G# A# C.

Regardless of whether you come from a classical, Jazz, or any other background, you should make the effort to familiarise yourself with the concepts and terminology of these two traditions. Each one has its own unique advantages and disadvantages, and there is much to be gained through being able to access the wealth of instructional, theoretical and analytical material available in both of these approaches.

The next example uses slash chords to provide inversions of these original chords. Notice how their upper notes, in contrast to the first version, form a melodic contour that ascends by tones and semitones, from the G on the third fret of the first string, up to the C on the eighth fret.

One of the less obvious advantages of using slash chords is that they have a harmonic ambiguity that allows these easily memorised chord shapes to be adapted to many different situations. Placing an A beneath a C triad might suggest an Am7 or an inverted C6. However, this voicing could also, depending on the context in which it is placed, serve as an incomplete C13. Adding a D beneath a C triad might suggest a D11, a D9sus4, an inverted C9 or Cmaj9, or even an inverted Em7b13, and so on.

It is also important to realise that the same chords can have different musical meanings depending upon whether we are hearing them in a tonal, modal or atonal context. For example, a D/C chord can function as a dominant seventh chord in the keys of G Major or Minor, as a tri-tone substitute for an Ab7 in the keys of Db Major or Minor, or as a secondary dominant in numerous other keys. On the other hand, it works very well as a tonic chord for the C Lydian mode, or for the C Lydian Augmented mode.[47]

The final subject that I would like to deal with in this chapter is a sort of mirror image of the strategies so far discussed. Rather than extracting melodic material from chords, it is also very useful to be able to extract harmonic material from melodies.

This approach is of particular use in modal improvising, or in freer situations where there are no clearly established harmonic patterns or fixed chord types. However, it can also provide

---

47   The third mode of A Melodic Minor.

alternative, often strikingly beautiful harmonies, in songs and pieces that already have a clearly defined harmonic structure. I have used this approach when playing everything from folk songs and Jazz standards, through to completely improvised pieces.

Ex.39 is intended to give just a taste of the potential of this approach in the hope that it will encourage you to include it in your own music.

I have written out this excerpt for two guitars. You will notice that, in each bar, the notes used to construct the chords in the second guitar part, are made up exclusively from the notes that form the melody, played by the first guitar. I have transposed some of these notes by an octave to create a satisfying tessitura,[48] and to ensure smoother voice leading between the chords.

I suggest that you record, or ask someone else to play the melody whilst you play the written chords.[49] Once you become familiar with the melodies shape, you might try varying the way that you interpret these chords. Try breaking them up into smaller fragments, adding more rhythmic interest and space. (See below.)

---

48   Texture.
49   I find my Boss RC-20 Loop Station is an invaluable aid when practising this sort of thing on my own.

As, I hope, this chapter has made clear; harmony and melody are closely interlinked with one another. Melody notes that are allowed to ring above and below each other become chords. The notes of chords that are stretched out in succession become melodic. Plucking the strings with the fingers seems to highlight this relationship very directly. This, for me is one of the most appealing aspects of this way of playing.

As improvisers, we cannot hope to bring the same rigor and precision to harmonic parts as can be achieved by a composer, who can take as long as he or she likes to experiment and perfect every single bar. However, improvisation compensates for this weakness by preserving freshness and spontaneity, allowing the music to continually evolve and change. This means that a piece of music always has the potential to become something much more than it might have been, had it remained fixed for ever, as a rigid composition.

Rhythmic Development

Many books, teachers, and students, devote a great deal of time to developing the use of chords and scales, and almost entirely neglect the development of rhythmic skills. This is unfortunate, as guitarists in general, and those from a classical background in particular, often seem to have a weakness in this area.[50]

The following exercises are intended to give some guidance on how I continue to address this problem in my own playing and that of my students.

Ex.40 Play the following examples using the suggested right hand fingers using both rest and free stroke. Use a metronome, starting slowly and gradually increase the tempo until you reach around 120 bpm. Rather than being over concerned with speed, you should concentrate on articulating the notes with precision and on achieving a good, solid tone. Repeat each example over and over again until it can be played without any feeling of hesitation or strain.

---

50   John Williams, with his customary insight and honesty, recommends, in a recent interview, that the majority of classical guitarists would benefit from listening to the American fingerstyle guitarist Leo Kottke, more than their more familiar role models. He has, on several occasions been critical of classical players who blindly model themselves on the playing of Segovia who tended to impose an indiscriminate 'Romantic' rubato time feel on everything he played, regardless of the stylistic demands of the music. John was drawing attention to the way in which many classical guitarists, because of their training and background, exhibit some difficulty in being rhythmically accurate and expressive.

Pat Metheny, in his workshops, regularly highlights timing problems in the playing of many otherwise highly accomplished Jazz players. He recommends careful work with a metronome, using rapid semi- quaver triplet subdivisions of the beat to develop accurate articulation.

The following example takes the same rhythm, and applies it to an ascending and descending 'E shape' G Major scale. Practice the same pattern, using all of the suggested right hand fingerings.

Now use the same approach with the other four CAGED Major scale fingerings. Once you have done this, you might try adapting these scales to include all of their associated modes, along with the twelve harmonic and melodic minor scales, and their modes as well.

I have only shown four out of many possible right hand variations. Once you get the hang of these, I suggest that you try some of your own. You might also try accenting one or two selected notes to develop individual finger independence and to add rhythmic variety.

Practising in this way facilitates the transformation of scales, (what we might regard as the 'raw materials', or 'building blocks' of music) into actual music. This approach works just as well with arpeggios and, as shown in the following exercises, with intervals and chords as well.

Ex.41 Takes the same rhythm as Ex.40 and applies it to two melodic scale patterns, from two different keys, on the first string. I have indicated only one of the suggested right hand fingerings for each example but you should play both examples using at least some of the other alternatives.

You could also try inventing your own variations to work with. I suggest that you write them out and memorise them, so that you can concentrate on placing them accurately against the metronome, without the added complication of wondering about what comes next. The idea here, is to internalise these ideas to the point when you are able to unconsciously recall them when improvising, using them as frameworks on which to structure new phrases and variations.

Close study of the music of all great improvisers reveals that they often utilise favourite musical patterns and gestures, which are adapted to the needs of the moment through transposition, rhythmic metamorphosis, etc. It would be wrong to imagine that the use of these 'signature licks', or patterns, detracts from the originality or inventiveness of the musician in question, as they are an essential, part of their own unique, personal voice.

Ex.42 takes these examples a stage further. I have retained the same rhythmic pattern as before but this time I have distributed the notes across the first *two* strings.

This example uses a combination of right hand fingering patterns derived from Ex.40 and 41. I hope that you can now begin to appreciate the need for the wide variety of fingering patterns suggested in these exercises. What we are trying to achieve is the ability to use any combination of right hand fingers, across any combination of strings, in a spontaneous and uninhibited manner. We need to develop this technique to the point that we can respond automatically to our musical ideas, as they arise.

Ex.43 again takes the same rhythmic pattern, but this time applies across strings one, two and three.

Ex.44 applies it across the first four strings.

Ex.45 shows the same rhythmic pattern across the first five strings. (This example is in more of a Jazz style. I have included the chord symbols to show as clearly as possible, the relationship between the CAGED chord shapes, the pre determined rhythm, and the resulting melody.)

Ex.46 and finally across all six strings.

The next group of exercises take a simple rhythmic idea, and develops it, step by step, into a larger, more complex structure. It might be useful for you to revise the intervallic aspects of Motivic Improvisation in the Improvising With Motives chapter, as there is a fundamental relationship between these, and the following rhythmic strategies.

Ex.47 Try clapping, or playing on one string, the following phrase, at a fairly slow tempo.

I have now taken things a little further, by repeating the same phrase, but this time modifying it by shortening the first crotchet in the second bar. Notice the way in which this simple variation engages the attention, propelling our interest forward towards the next musical event. (A good improvisation or composition should unfold like a story, engaging our interest as it moves from one part to the next.)

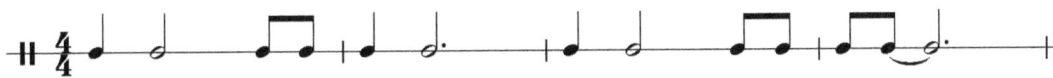

The next phrase (bars 5 and 6) looks very different from the first two. However, closer inspection reveals that I have now sub divided the notes at the beginning and end of each bar, and retained the distinctive longer notes in the centre. This develops the rhythmic 'story' further, without losing its underlying continuity. This increase in activity creates a growing tension, leading up to the next phrase.

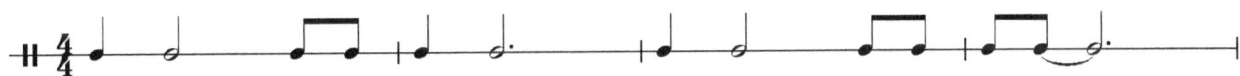

This is followed a shorter, one bar phrase that sill faintly echoes the original alternation of longer notes flanked by shorter ones, but with the note values halved, and the rhythmic activity much more busy, and intense.

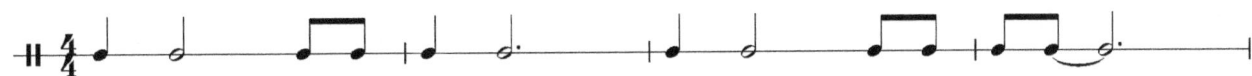

The next bar takes the last two semiquavers, and quaver rest, on the last beat of bar 7, and repeats them. This creates the effect of the gathering momentum, accumulated in the previous bars, being reined in.

The passage continues in bars 9 and 10, by returning to a variation of the first phrase.

That is followed in bars 11 and 12, by yet another variation.

The phrase in bars 9 and 10 is repeated in bars 11 and 12.

13

[musical notation]

The passage is then concluded with a reprise of the stuttering 'reining in' figure from bar 8, followed by a concluding semibreve.

[musical notation]

5

[musical notation]

9

[musical notation]

13

[musical notation]

Now you should try taking this rhythmic pattern, and apply the strategies outlined in Ex's. 40 to 46.

The capacity for this type of musical inventiveness, especially in a spontaneous, improvisational situation, obviously varies from person to person. There seem to be several determining factors that affect our ability in this regard. The first and most significant is how well we have been taught. This includes the teacher's own background, expectations, and skill, and whether we have had positive learning experiences that have built our self-confidence rather than undermined it.

Another important factor is the extent and depth to which we have listened to the music of others.

Accents are an essential element in rhythmic development. I find it very useful to relate the use of accents to the way in which we speak. Emphasising different words within a sentence can radically alter its meaning. For example, if we take the phrase 'Is this your banana?' and stress only the first word, (*IS* this your banana?) we infer a very different meaning than if we put the accent on the second word. (Is *THIS* your banana?) A similar thing happens if we accent either of the last two words.

One of the things that I have always admired about singers like Billie Holiday or Bob Dylan is the way in which they continually improvise new accents and phrasing, throwing unexpected and fresh perspectives on a songs lyrics. Their ability to manipulate meaning, and play with language is analogous to the way in which a Jazz instrumentalist approaches the melody of a familiar standard.

Jazz veterans routinely advise students wishing to play standards to learn the songs original lyrics for precisely this reason.[51] A much loved melody can be radically altered and still remain familiar to an audience, so long as they can still follow its underlying shape. What is more, an accomplished improviser to should be able to take any familiar melody and develop it through successive choruses, in such a way that the audience experiences it as a logically unfolding musical 'story'.

One of the things that I don't like to hear in a Jazz performance is when the band play the melody in a routine way, and then continue for the rest of the piece trying to dazzle me with their technical prowess, creating unconnected, increasingly hysterical lines that bear no relationship to the original theme. Eberhard Weber once, memorably referred to this unfortunate tendency as 'playing for victory'.

This subject could fill a whole book in its own right. In the context of this present volume, I will limit myself to just a few simple examples in the hope that these will suffice to stimulate your own interest and exploration.

Ex.48 shows a musical phrase that derives its rhythmic shape from the question 'is this your banana?' with the accents on different notes. Once you get used to the sound and feel of each accent, try applying the strategies of transposition, ornamentation, variation, diminution and augmentation, detailed in the 'Improvising With Motives' chapter, above.

Any verbal phrase, or sentence, can be transformed into a rhythmic phrase or melody. The opening bar of Paul McCartney's famous song 'Yesterday' started out as 'scrambled eggs'. Everything from Gregorian chant, to Hebridean Psalm singing, and Scat Singing, uses the rhythms and patterns of language as a model for rhythmic and melodic invention. Instrumental composers as well as songwriters, from time immemorial, have used words and phrases to generate new musical ideas.

51   See for example, 'Thinking In Jazz' by Paul F Berliner.

Perhaps the best, most widely available example of this approach, by an improvising musician, is to be found on John Coltrane's famous album 'A Love Supreme'. The fourth and final section of the suite, entitled 'Psalm', is clearly based on the words of the accompanying poem. (Printed in the sleeve notes.) These can be read along with John's beautiful improvised melody as though they were song lyrics.[52]

Clearly there are also many practical advantages for improvisers in this approach. Snippets of imagined or overheard conversation, lines from a poem or favourite song lyric, or even phrases from a book or newspaper can provide fertile material from which to work.

I have also found the reverse of this process to be useful when helping students interpret written rhythms that they are having problems with. In this case as an alternative to counting out the offending passage I will, instead, invent an appropriate spoken phrase. For some reason I usually use a culinary theme for this! Many is the time when a 'Mushroom Foo Yung', or a 'Paprika Chicken served with chips on the side', will help a student break through an otherwise impenetrable barrier to their progress, and at the same time reduce my own stress levels.

Another important element in creating and developing rhythmic ideas is the use of space. Without space, there can be no shape. One of the most common mistakes made by less experienced improvisers is to play continually. For the listener this is the musical equivalent of being faced with page after page of dense text, with no gaps between the words, punctuation, paragraphs, chapter headings, and so on.

One of the most difficult things to do when improvising is to keep an objective overview of the music being created. We can easily fall into the trap of becoming fixated on what is coming next, and loose sight of the way in which all the previous ideas need to be shaped into a coherent and satisfying whole. Guitarists in particular tend to get locked into compulsively repeating learnt fingering patterns, relying on 'motor', muscular, finger memory, rather than more musical considerations. Using space in a creative way, to punctuate our ideas, allows us time for reflection and re assessment, and to shape the form of the emerging music.

Space can be introduced into a piece of music in many different ways. The most obvious of which is to include rests or long sustained notes. Other strategies might include the use of quiet, repetitive sequences of notes that introduce a feeling of stasis, or the use of harmonics, pizzicato, creating percussive sounds on the guitar's body, ambient electronic effects etc.

Ex.49 shows how rests or ties can be used to create space in an improvised line, making a more interesting passage of music.

This example is based on an Ab Lydian mode and is made up of continuous semi-quavers. Each group of four semi-quavers moves around an interval of a third, which is built on different steps of the mode. (See Ex.8)

I have included a bass line to reinforce the modal sound of this passage. It works just as well, and is easier to play if you omit this part and just play the uppermost melodic line.

---

52   See also 'John Coltrane, His Life and Music', by Lewis Porter.

I have now inserted four (quaver length) rests, at key points in this passage. Notice how the previously rather drab line is enlivened by the introduction of these spaces.

Here is the same passage again. This time I have introduced tied notes, instead of rests, in the same places.

Ex.50 again introduces more space into an improvised line, this time by using a quiet, repetitive figure inserted in between the notes of the melody.

The uppermost line should be played louder (*mf*) than the lower line, (*p*) to emphasise the distinction between the melody and its accompaniment. The lower line is played with a 'palm mute',[53] again to contrast the separate parts.

This same idea could be used in reverse, with the melodic activity taking place in the bass part, and the softer, repetitive figure, being played in the upper line.

Ex.51 demonstrates a similar strategy, but this time uses un-pitched notes (indicated with the 'x' note heads on the extra staff) to create space, and to develop the piece rhythmically.

The guitar can easily be used as a 'percussion instrument', and there are many different ways that we can produce these un-pitched sounds.

Try playing the following passage, firstly without the extra line. When you are comfortable with this part, try adding the 'percussion' part, using one, or more of the following techniques.

 a. Tamboura. (Striking the strings with the side of the thumb. The edge of the nail can also be used to highlight specific strings.)
 b. Golpe. (Striking the bridge using the side of the thumb, fingertips, or the side of the hand.)
 c. Tapping various parts of the guitars neck and body with the fingers, fingernails, thumb, palm, knuckles, etc.
 d. Lightly strumming across the strings above the nut, using the fingernails of the right, or left hand.

---

53   I prefer this term to the more traditional 'pizzicato' or 'appagado', as it is a more precise description of the technique, as used by guitarists. Pizzicato is an instruction for bowed string players to pluck, (or sometimes snap,) the string with their fingers rather than to use a bow. My trusty Collins musical dictionary doesn't include the word appagado which was, I think, suggested by Segovia as an alternative to pizzicato, in his efforts to gain the same status for the guitar as for other 'classical' instruments.

I have tried to vary the style of these exercises, to emphasise the way in which almost any rhythmic idea can be adapted to numerous different musical situations. Many Jazz teachers encourage their students to memorize 'licks'. These are often taken from transcriptions from recordings of famous players. They are chosen to enable the student to compile a repertoire of ready-made ideas that fit over common Jazz chord progressions. Indian classical musicians and others often adopt similar strategies.

Improvisation treatises of the seventeenth, eighteenth, and early nineteenth centuries, written by such eminent figures as C P E Bach, and Carl Czerny recommended the memorisation of cadences, harmonised scales, and 'Movimenti'[54] Great emphasis was also placed on memorising the numerous varieties of ornamentation, on transposition, and on the variation and re combination of pre learnt patterns. Teachers from this period, like

---

54   'Special moves', including modulatory progressions, chromatic notes, complex bass lines, etc. These would be memorised by the student in all keys, and then adapted for use during the actual performance.

their present day counterparts, also provided models of ideal improvisations in the form of transcribed preludes and cadenzas. Aspiring musicians, then, as now, were expected to assimilate key elements of technique, structure and style through the study and memorisation of these pieces. There are, for example, over fifty surviving transcriptions, that Mozart wrote out for his own students.

There are clear advantages in this approach. Students learn a vocabulary that incorporates all of the necessary stylistic hallmarks of their chosen musical genre. They learn when, how, and why to apply specific tried and tested ideas that are known to work. In spite of these advantages many other musicians choose not to apply pre-learnt ideas, feeling that this can lead to a sort of 'music by numbers' approach.

Perhaps the best example of this polarisation of opinion is found in the heated debates between Jazz musicians from the late fifties onwards. Those who identified themselves with the established Be Bop and Hard Bop styles often criticised the 'abandonment of swing', slower tempos, and less frequent chord changes, adopted by many Model and Free players. The implication, that this was due to their 'technical inadequacies', was more a product of the competitive, machismo Bop and Hard Bop culture than a fair criticism of their opponent's musical accomplishments.[55]

In response to these kind of attacks, the new wave of musicians were quick to draw attention to the increasing sterility of performers, mindlessly repeating the same formulaic ideas, with the only criteria of success being the speed at which these clichés could be churned out. They felt that the faster the tempos became, and the more overcrowded and frenetic the chord changes, the more improvisation was squeezed out in favour of pre-planned pyrotechnics.[56]

Many musicians abandoned the use of pre-learnt formulas in favour of a radical commitment to spontaneous improvisation, and in doing so managed to expand the possibilities of Jazz. Tempos were slowed down; asymmetric metres, such as 5/4, and 7/4, found their way from European and Indian classical music's into the mainstream of Jazz, and even (with Paul Desmond's 'Take Five') into the charts. Cecil Taylor, Eric Dolphy, John Coltrane, and others introduced increasingly complex sub-divisions of the pulse, superimposition of different metres, and in some cases, the abandonment of fixed metres all together, in favour of so called 'Energy Playing'.[57]

In my own music I tend to avoid using pre learnt ideas when improvising, although, as I mentioned earlier, I attach great value to making, learning, and studying transcriptions of the recorded work of other musicians. When practising, my aims are to nurture my technical confidence and fluency, and to enrich my vocabulary. To this end I try to draw inspiration and ideas from as wide a variety of different music as I can. I find that these diverse influences, whether from Classical, Jazz, Rock, Iranian music, or wherever, all leave an imprint. This imprint somehow seems to find expression as the music unfolds.[58]

---

55   Musicians on the receiving end of this type of criticism are in good company. A random list might include such luminaries as Miles Davis, Cecil Taylor, Don Cherry, Charlie Haden, Bill Frisell, Jim Hall, Ornette Coleman, Jan Garbarek, and many, many more.

56   Similar patterns of thought and behaviour seem to be playing themselves out in the various varieties of 'Metal', and other styles of Rock guitar playing at the moment.

57   See 'Free Jazz', by Ekkehardt Jost, and 'New Structures In Jazz And Improvised Music Since 1960', by Roger T Dean.

58   See 'Improvisation and Composition' chapter, above.

What we listen to and enjoy, is the key to understanding our own musical identity. No two people feel the same way about the same music. Our accumulated listening experience provides us with a unique reservoir of musical techniques, and expressive resources. These can, through hard work, become transmuted into a personal voice, that enables us to communicate our shared cultures, tastes, values, and passions to others in an original and meaningful way.

I often feel a little uncomfortable when I am listening to a musician who is adopting someone else's persona. Whether it is someone from the north of England assuming the accent and mannerisms of a Delta Blues singer, a rock guitarist in a 'tribute band' wearing the same cloths as their idol and mimicking him in every detail, or a Jazz musician dressing, playing and talking like someone from New York in the nineteen forties. While I often find myself admiring the skill and dedication of these people, in the end we must distinguish between music that is creative and music that is only re creative.

Form

Along with rhythm, melody, and harmony, form is one of the fundamental elements in music. Whilst sharing many points in common with written composition, the treatment of form in improvised music presents us with unique challenges.

We might define form as the way in which we structure a piece of music in a coherent and satisfying way, as it unfolds over time. In Jazz and Baroque music, for example, this challenge was, at first; solved in a straightforward way- the improvised section was based on the underlying harmony and structure of a chosen song, or, in the Baroque suite, a movement based on a popular dance.

Freer less structured improvisations could be included in a dance suite, as a Prelude. In Jazz, the equivalent to the prelude is the 'Intro'. This is usually a short improvisation that sets the mood for the forthcoming piece of music by freely drawing on its distinctive rhythmic, harmonic, or melodic elements.

In shorter pieces, the need for variety and shape is not as critical. However, the longer a piece of music becomes, the need for a coherent formal design increases.

This can be seen in the evolution of European music, from the Baroque suite, which was made up of five or six short, popular dances, unified by one key, to the later development of the large symphonic forms of Classical and Romantic music. In the USA Jazz composers like Duke Ellington, Charles Mingus, John Coltrane, Miles Davis, and Gil Evans, each, in their own unique way found solutions to the challenges of creating longer, more complex works that superseded the limitations of the traditional thirty two bar chorus, or the twelve bar blues form.

The development of successive generations of recording formats has also had a significant impact on the form of Jazz. Louis Armstrong would often improvise thirty or more blues choruses during a single live performance. However, the old 78rpm format limited the length of pieces to around two and a half minutes. Things improved with the introduction of the 33rpm LP that allowed people like John Coltrane and Miles Davis to introduce individual pieces or sections of up to around twenty minutes. The more recent introduction of the CD extended the potential length of pieces to over an hour, roughly the length of one of the longer late Romantic symphonic works. With the ever-expanding possibilities of each successive generation of new technology it will be interesting to see how musicians will respond to the possibilities of recording even longer improvised works.[59]

It is also worthwhile to study the way in which other cultures have approached this challenge. Improvisation has a central role in the music of India and Iran. Both of these traditions have developed sophisticated strategies for the formal organisation of long, improvised, musical performances. These are of great potential value to those of us who are interested in incorporating new influences into our own music.

Ex.52 details some of the principal forms used in 'Classical Music' over the last couple of centuries, along with a rather simplistic depiction of the ordering of each successive musical theme. (AABC etc.)

---

59   Composers, with the aid of computers, seem to be ahead of the game here. Brian Eno has created pieces designed to last for several days, and I recently heard of a piece being performed in a church in France that is scheduled to last for over a century. Improvised music is, of course reliant on the stamina of the performer, however Indian classical Ragas can sometimes last for several hours, and some forms of improvised African communal music can last a whole day.

Simple Binary	A B
Binary	A A B
Song Form	A A B A (ABA)
Minuet Form	A A B A B A
Minuet Trio	A A B A B A C C D C D C A B A
Scherzo Trio	A A B B C C D D A B
Arch Form	A B C B A
Sonata Form	Introduction. Exposition. Cadence. Development. Recapitulation. Coda.
Rondo Form	A B A C A D etc.
Rhapsody	A B C D E etc
Fantasy	Totally Free.

In composed music the repetition, variation and contrast of the various sections is usually fairly self-evident. In improvised music, what constitutes a particular section can include a whole spectrum of material. This might range from a short rhythmic or melodic motive, or a single chord or riff- through to a completely notated melody, with a fixed sequence of chords. For the improviser this material, and the layout of subsequent sections are seen as a point of departure. One of the primary aims of this book is to give you a broad range of practical strategies for creating music from any point within this spectrum.

Variation of a pre-composed passage can be achieved in many different ways. For example;

    a. The melody remains unchanged, whilst the harmony or contrapuntal parts are varied.[60] (When playing a Jazz standard, this would include altering the bass line, chord substitutions and extensions, as well as the rhythmic interplay between the drums and other band members)

    b. The harmony, or contrapuntal parts remain unchanged, whilst the melody is varied.

    c. The melody is varied through ornamentation.

    d. Free (motivic) variation.

As improvisers, we can also choose whether to work with a pre-determined form, or whether to allow the music to shape itself, as it actually unfolds. When listening back to recordings of my own completely improvised pieces, I am sometimes surprised by their underlying coherence and symmetry, factors of which I had little conscious awareness of, whilst I was actually performing.[61] In this situation, my main concern is to maintain continuity, and a sense of purpose and direction.

New sections, or phases emerge when the old one has run its course. This process should happen naturally, avoiding any tendency to force or rush things. There is often a period of transition between different parts of an improvisation. This might include the gradual breaking down of the previous section, and gradual emergence of a new idea from the fragments of the old. On the other hand, it might just as easily include the introduction

---

60   Listen, for example, to 'Nefertiti' by Miles Davis.
61   See 'Improvisation and Composition' chapter, above.

of sharply contrasting material that introduces a completely new energy into the music, sending it into a different and unexpected direction.[62]

'Mistakes', or unintended notes can be very useful here. Out of necessity, we can either choose to ignore a mistake, regarding it as a minor blemish, or we can incorporate it as a new, albeit unexpected element in the performance.[63] All improvisers will be well acquainted with both options! Experience tends to confirm the fact that it is often 'mistakes' that can lead to the best bits of a piece, and that more accomplished improvisers, whilst not exactly welcoming such occurrences, certainly don't fear them.

The form of an improvised piece of music does not have to be delineated only in terms of its constituent musical features. An alternative way of structuring things is to give performance directions to individual players. These might range from very general instructions, like 'play freely for about a minute, and then pause for about thirty seconds...etc.' To much more precise instructions, specifying, for example particular keys, chords, scales, rhythmic patterns, dynamics, and so on. This strategy is very useful as it represents a sort of middle ground between free playing, and a more detailed, written score.

The language used to direct musicians in these types of pieces is often, out of necessity, a bit vague and subjective. This can be regarded as a strength or as a weakness. A sentence like 'Continue to repeat the pattern, gradually letting it fragment and decay into a three second silence.' (Ex.53.) Is detailed enough to give shape to the music without restricting the improvisers creative flow. The direction, (from section 7 of the same piece,) 'Select a short sequence of triads that evoke a pleasing, peaceful, feeling.' Is, even more subjective, but enables the performer to respond to the moment in a uniquely personal way.

Ex.53 is an example of this approach, composed for solo guitar. The aim of this piece is to contrast the rather dark, soulful opening, with the gently optimistic ending. All of the guitars formidable advantages, with regard to tone colour, should be exploited to the full.

---

62   This is one of the advantages of improvising with others, and one of the disadvantages of improvising solo, where we can only look to ourselves for new ideas.

63   See, for example, references to musical 'saves' in Paul F Berliners 'Thinking In Jazz'.

1
Improvise a slow, dark, rubato melody, in the E Phrygian mode, restricting yourself to the three lower strings. (Approx. 1 to 1 ½ minutes.)

2
Focus on one chosen note, on each of these three strings, and gradually sustain them, until they form a chord.

3
Slowly introduce a consistent metre and tempo, creating a quick, repeated arpeggio consisting of either five, or eight quavers to the bar. Repeat this new pattern until it is firmly established.

4
Abandoning the E Phrygian mode, but retaining the same parallel, left hand fingering and right hand arpeggio pattern, move this chord vertically, to different positions on the neck, creating a fluid, shifting, kaleidoscope of notes, with no fixed tonal centre. (Approx. 1 min.)

5
Settle this chord's 'root' on to the note 'A' on the fifth fret on the sixth string. Continue to repeat the pattern, gradually letting it fragment and decay into a three second silence. During this time, select a major or minor key that contains the three notes of this chord.

6
Introduce random first and second inversion triads (from the chosen key), a semibreve in length, played in 4/4 time at a moderate tempo. These triads should be played softly, on the first four strings only.

7
Select a short sequence of triads that evoke a pleasing, peaceful, feeling. Combine both scale and arpeggio notes to improvise a new, simple, diatonic melody.

8
After repeating this melody a few times, gradually slow it down, until it resolves softly to a final tonic triad.

Ex.54 applies this same strategy, this time composed for a trio consisting of guitar, double bass, and drums. A copy of the score should be given to each player, with his or her own part marked with a highlighter pen. The challenge here is to achieve a smooth, seamless transition between each section, and to maintain harmonic and melodic coherence without a clearly established tonal centre.

1
GUITAR - Improvise a medium fast, 'comping' pattern, using parallel Major 9th chords.

2
BASS – After about thirty seconds, improvise a walking bass line, responding to and interacting with the guitar.

3
DRUMS – After about thirty seconds, accompany the bass and guitar on the ride cymbal.

4
GUITAR – Wait until the bass and drums have established good rapport, and then begin to improvise a fast, fluid, melodic line.
BASS – Gradually abandon the walking bass line, and begin to develop more melodic, contrapuntal ideas, complementing the guitar.
DRUMS – Accompany the guitar, and bass, gradually incorporating more of the kit as the music develops.

5
DRUMS – Keeping an even volume, gradually increase the level of activity until you are cutting across the guitar and bass, as if asserting yourself in a conversation.
GUITAR - Gradually give way to the drums, eventually lapsing into a short period of silence.
BASS – Gradually give way to the drums, eventually lapsing into silence.

6
DRUMS – Over a period of about sixty seconds, gradually reduce the level of activity, eventually returning to the same pattern on the ride cymbal as you established in section three.

7
GUITAR – Wait until the drums have re established the ride cymbal pattern, then return to the 'comping' pattern based on the same parallel movement of Major 9th chords as section one.

8
GUITAR – Gradually reduce your volume, eventually ending on an A Maj 9th Chord.
BASS – Accompany the guitars final A Maj 9th chord with a long bowed note that gradually decays into silence.
DRUMS – Gradually reduce your volume, falling silent on the final chord.

Conclusion

Writing this book has brought home to me, more than ever, just how complex a task improvisation actually is. I have been as conscious of what, for the sake of clarity, I have had to leave out, as much as what I have chosen to include. The material contained in any one of these short chapters could easily have been expanded into a whole book in its own right.

The guitar lacks the dynamic range of brass instruments. In comparison to the piano, its harmonic options are quite limited; it cannot match the speed of the saxophone, or the soaring, sustained melodies of bowed instruments like the cello or violin. However, in a unique way it is able to combine echoes of all of these different qualities into one voice. In the right hands, it can truly become an orchestra in miniature. By exploiting these advantages, fingerstyle guitarists can create their own very individual approaches to the art of improvisation.

Although I have only scratched the surface of this subject, and that there are several lifetimes work here, you should not let this discourage you. Some of the very greatest improvised music has been created using only the simplest ideas and resources. Complexity for its own sake is never aesthetically satisfying. We should play within the boundaries of our own limitations, gradually learning to expand these boundaries through practise, experience, and experimentation. Rather than allowing ourselves to become side-tracked by illusionary feelings of competitiveness or destructive self-criticism we should retain a sense of the joy of making music, striving for what is beautiful, meaningful and poetic.

APPENDIX

THE CAGED SYSTEM

Part One: Major Scales, Tonic Chords, and Arpeggios

The CAGED system is a practical way of visualising chords, arpeggios, scales, and keys across the whole guitar fingerboard. It is useful for both improvisation, and for sight-reading, and is, like all of the best systems, based on a simple idea.

It takes its name from the following five basic first position chord shapes:

Ex.1

Each of these five chord shapes is a framework that can be adapted to build numerous other chords, arpeggios, and scales. The beauty of this approach is that it provides us with an obvious visual, aural, and tactile relationship between any given chord and its related arpeggio or scale. Furthermore, as I will demonstrate below, these shapes all inter-lock with each other, producing a network of familiar patterns across the entire fingerboard.

It is not my intention to present a chord/scale/arpeggio dictionary. The following examples represent only a fraction of the available material. These examples are drawn from the most commonly used shapes, and reflect my own personal preferences and habits. I would encourage you to explore and personalise the way in which you use these ideas, particularly with regard to fingerings, and chord voicings.

The word CAGED spells out the five basic shapes *in order*, as they are moved up the fingerboard. For example, a C major chord in each of the five positions (including a C shape C chord one, octave above the original first position chord) would look like this:

Ex.2

The final chord, in the twelfth position, mirrors the first position C chord an octave below. It is the same C shape but, out of necessity, utilises all four left hand fingers. This is because of the absence of the available open strings when it is played in the first position.

Each of these five chords can be seen as a sort of skeleton, on which can be hung the surrounding scale, along with its related arpeggio.

Ex.3 shows a C shape, first position C Major scale, arpeggio, and Cmaj7 chord.

You should thoroughly familiarise yourself with this and the following chord/scale/ arpeggio relationships.

Ex.4 takes this same C shape and moves it up two frets, so that it becomes a 'C shape', *D Major scale, arpeggio, or chord*. The first finger now plays what, in the first position would have been open strings, requiring us to use the fourth finger in place of the third, and so on.

Once this transition has been made, the same fingerings can be relocated in different positions to play all twelve major keys.

Ex.5 applies the same idea to an A shape, A Major scale, an Amaj7 chord, and arpeggio.

When the A shape is moved up to higher positions that do not include open strings, there are two possible fingerings for the Major scale, its arpeggio, and chord. The first closely follows the first position shape, and starts with the first finger. The following example is in Bb Major:

This fingering is essential in the first position, and works well enough in higher positions.

A more comfortable fingering, is the following one that I have shown in the second position, in the key of C Major. This fingering, unlike the previous A shape example, doesn't work in the first position. Every variation has its own distinct advantages and disadvantages. This becomes self evident later on when we start adapting these Major scales into other modes and scales.

It is also worth noting how different fingerings affect our melodic choices when improvising, and the way in which they can also facilitate our interpretation of written music.

Along with the Cmaj7 chord/arpeggio, I also have included, in the last three bars, of this example, a common voicing for a Cmaj9 chord/arpeggio. This illustrates the relationship between this scale fingering, and just two, of its many potentially available tonic chords and arpeggios. The fact that these chords can be found right under the fingers provides a valuable insight into working not only with chord shapes, but also when applying all of the other improvisational strategies that I have outlined earlier in this book.

Ex.6 shows a first position, G shape, G Major scale, along with its tonic, two octave, major seventh arpeggio. I have also included voicings for a Gmaj7, and G6 chord. I suggest that you spend some time experimenting with as many tonic major type chords, and their arpeggios, as possible. Try finding, for example, different ways to play 6th, 6/9, add9, sus2, sus4 and major chords. Try breaking the large six-string chord into smaller triads. (You will find root, first and second inversion triads all contained within this one shape.[64])

These shapes, moved up two frets give us the following G shape, A Major scale, arpeggio, and chords. I prefer to stretch up to the G# on the fourth string, rather than move out of position, by reaching for it with my first finger on the third string. Once you are used to this it feels perfectly comfortable, and has the advantage of maintaining, if desired, a first finger barre. It also preserves the original G shape, and makes it easy to adapt.[65] I also recommend that, when possible, you stretch between the second and fourth fingers, as indicated, rather than the more awkward stretch between the third and fourth fingers.

---

64   See 'Chord Scales' chapter, above.

65   For example, if we lower this G# (along with the one on the first string) to G, we create a very useful and comfortable, two octave, G Mixolydian mode or G7 arpeggio. (See below.)

Ex.7 shows the E shape- the fourth of the CAGED patterns.

The E shape can begin on either the open E string. Alternatively you can visualise these shapes in their movable forms, as starting from the note F on the first fret, (with the first finger), or from the note Gb on the second fret, (starting with the second finger).

The open string, E Major scale, Maj7 arpeggio, and chord, looks like this:

This second version of the E shape starts with the first finger. It is, perhaps, most useful when the shape is adapted to minor and dominant seventh type fingerings. It is also the only practical choice, when the scale or arpeggio starts on F on the first fret.

The final version, starting with the second finger is most useful for Major Scales, and Lydian type modes, along with their arpeggios and chords.

You will notice that I have given three shapes for the E shape maj7 chord. The Emaj7 chord utilises open strings. The Fmaj7 is the same shape moved up a fret employing a first finger barre, whilst the Gbmaj7, utilises individual fingers to create a flexible four note version of this same shape. These are only a few of the possibilities, as before you should try adding ninths, sixths, etc.

I apologise for the rather difficult key signature in this example! It would have been easier to show you this pattern in the much more guitar friendly key of G Major, one fret higher. However, I wanted to illustrate some of the many advantages of this way of thinking.

All three of these examples are in the first position. If we now include an A shape, A, Bb, and B Major scale, we have six, first position, Major scales, arpeggios and chords.

Adding D shape, (see below) D Major and Eb Major patterns, a C shape, C Major and Db Major patterns, along with G shape, G Major, and Ab Major patterns, *gives us all twelve Major Scales, Arpeggios, and tonic major chords in the first position.* This inter-related network of keys, arpeggios, chords, and fingerings remains consistent as it is moved to different positions on the fingerboard. The shapes remain the same, only their names change.

The advantages of this, whether sight reading, improvising, transcribing, or editing and fingering new pieces, should by now be obvious!

The last CAGED pattern is the D shape.

Ex.8 outlines this pattern in its original, first position, utilising open strings. I have then moved these same shapes up one fret, creating an Eb Major, scale, arpeggio, and maj7 chord.

Here are the same shapes, raised one fret to create an Eb Major scale, arpeggio, and maj7 chord

Although this pattern encompasses only a minor tenth, above the fourth string tonic, I never the less, find it to be very useful. Bear in mind that, like all of these shapes, this one can also be extended *below* the lowest available tonic, to locate other modes, arpeggios and chords. I also find this pattern very easy to visualise, and adapt.

Part Two: Locating The Modes, Arpeggios, and Seventh Chords, Contained Within The Five CAGED Major Scale Shapes

Each of these five, Major Scale (Ionian Mode) patterns contains six other Modes, along with their associated arpeggios and chords. Once again, I have chosen to use seventh chords to illustrate the way in which they relate to the scale shapes. It should be born in mind, that there are, of course, many alternative possibilities, all of which should be thoroughly explored.

Ex.9 shows the fingering for each of these seven modes, along with their tonic chords and arpeggios, in all five CAGED shapes.

This material, in the form that it is presented here, is, out of necessity, rather dry and uninspiring. Try to remember that familiarisation with this material is only the first step. It is your own responsibility to take the second step, and transform this information into music.

Modes from the C shape major scale pattern

These shapes lie easily under the fingers. As in the following shapes, I have shown each mode as either a one octave, or where possible, without moving out of position, a two octave scale.

To maximise the notes available, in as many modes as possible I have extended all of the basic CAGED shapes to include notes that can be reached below the tonic, without having to shift position. In this C shape for example, I can reach down as low as the F# on the sixth string, which enables me to play a two octave, E shape, F# Phrygian mode.

It is, of course possible, in many instances, to include notes that extend above and below the indicated one and two octave scales and arpeggios.

D Major/Ionian. (C Shape)

E Dorian. (D Shape)

F# Phrygian Mode. (E Shape)

G Lydian Mode. (E Shape)

A Mixolydian Mode. (G Shape)

B Aeolian Mode. (A Shape)

C# Locrian Mode. (A Shape)

Modes from the A Shape scale pattern

I have shown only the versions of the A (and later on E) shape patterns that start with the second finger. As I mentioned earlier, those that start with the first finger tend to be more useful when playing minor and mixolydian/dominant seventh type patterns. Some of these will be shown in the third and final part of this appendix.

D Major/Ionian Mode. (A Shape)

E Dorian Mode. (C Shape)

F# Phrygian Mode. (D Shape)

G Lydian Mode. (D Shape)

A Mixolydian Mode. (E Shape)

B Aeolian Mode. (G Shape)

C# Locrian Mode. (A Shape)

Modes from the G Shape scale pattern

Don't be put off by some of the more difficult stretches. If the left hand is properly positioned, spanning five frets should present no problems. Because of the anatomy of the hand, I usually try to stretch between the first and second, rather than between the third and fourth fingers, however different situations will demand different solutions.

Although some of these fingerings are a little awkward, they are all useful. Each is an essential part of the overall picture, although I am sure that you, like me will tend to favour some shapes more than others.

A Major/Ionian Mode. (G Shape)

B Dorian Mode. (A Shape)

C# Phrygian Mode. (C Shape)

D Lydian Mode. (C Shape)

F# Aeolian Mode. (E Shape)

G# Locrian Mode. (E Shape)

Modes from the E Shape scale pattern

As in the A shape examples above, I have shown only the version of this fingering that starts with the second finger.

G Major/Ionian Mode. (E Shape)

A Dorian Mode. (G Shape)

B Phrygian Mode. (A Shape)

C Lydian Mode. (A Shape)

D Mixolydian Mode. (C Shape)

E Aeolian Mode. (D Shape)

F# Locrian Mode. (E Shape)

Modes from the D Shape scale pattern

Because this shape starts on the fourth string, most of the available modes are found on the fifth and sixth strings.

E Major/Ionian Mode. (D Shape)

F# Dorian Mode. (E Shape)

G# Phrygian Mode. (E Shape)

A Lydian Mode. (G Shape)

B Mixolydian Mode. (A Shape)

C# Aolian Mode. (A Shape)

D# locrian Mode. (C Shape)

Part Three: Adapting CAGED Shapes To Create Other Scales And Modes

These final examples are intended to demonstrate the practicality and flexibility of this system. The ability for guitarists to move smoothly through different tonal centres, by adjusting only one or two fingers, is obviously a huge advantage. These simple adaptations can also be easily related, aurally and visually, to their associated intervals, chords, and arpeggios.

Rather than show each scale or mode starting and ending on its tonic, as I did in the previous section, I have opted to show all of the available notes, above the tonic, without having to shift position.

You should be selective, focusing, at first, on patterns that are most accessible to you. However, I do recommend that you gradually acquaint yourself with all of the possibilities. It is important to acquire an overview of the overall concept, and you will find that even some of the less accessible shapes are useful when you select fragments, rather than trying to use the whole shape all the time.

Ex.10   Takes an E shape A major scale and, one finger at a time transforms it into its three parallel minor scales. I have also added an A Diminished Scale,[66] Whole Tone Scale, both starting with the first finger.

A Major. (E Shape)

A Melodic Minor. (E Shape)

A Harmonic Minor. (E Shape)

A Natural Minor/Aeolian Mode. (E Shape)

---

66   This is also called the Whole Tone/ Half Tone Scale, or the even longer- Double Diminished Octatonic Scale. (The same scale, starting from the G# would be called the Half Tone Whole Tone Scale.)

A Diminished/Whole Tone-Half Tone. (E Shape)

A Whole Tone. (E Shape)

The next two scales are alternative fingerings for these E shape, Diminished and whole Tone Scales, - both of which, because of their symmetrical shapes, I find very useful.

A Diminished/Whole Tone Half Tone Scale. (E Shape) Alternative Fingering.

A Whole Tone Scale. (E Shape) Alternative Fingering.

Ex.11 adapts a C shape, E Major scale, into an E Melodic Minor scale, followed by an E Harmonic Minor scale, again, by staying in the same position, and adjusting one finger at a time.

E Major. (C Shape)   E Melodic Minor. (C Shape)

E Harmonic Minor. (C Shape)

This adaptation starts on the sixth degree of the same C shape E Major scale, creating a C# Natural Minor/ Aeolian mode. The seventh of this scale is raised, to form a C# Harmonic Minor scale.

C# Natural Minor/Aeolian Mode. (A Shape)

C# Harmonic Minor. (A Shape)

This final adaptation is again derived from the same C shape, E Major scale as before. However, this time I have taken the second step of this scale as my root, creating a D shape, F# Dorian mode, starting with the first finger on the fourth string. I then raise the seventh of this mode, to form a D shape, F# Melodic Minor scale.

F# Dorian Mode. (D Shape)

F# Melodic Minor. (D Shape)

By now, I am sure that you will have noticed that I could have achieved the same result by lowering the third step of a D shape, F# Major scale.

It is not my intention to detail all of the possibilities. This book would have to be substantially thicker if I did, and to quote Bill Evans, in a slightly different context, 'I wouldn't want to deprive you of the pleasure of discovering these things for yourself.'

www.ingramcontent.com/pod-product-compliance
Lightning Source LLC
Chambersburg PA
CBHW081136090426
42740CB00014BA/2878